**FAMILY FUTURES CONSORTIUM LIMITED.**
17 NEWINGTON GREEN.LONDON N16 9PU
TELEPHONE . 0207 241 0503.FAX 0207 923 1093
COMPANY REGISTRATION NO. 3571649.

A  NOT FOR PROFIT ORGANISATION

D1147532

# Where's Daddy?

*Separation and Your Child*

———

## JILL CURTIS AND VIRGINIA ELLIS

BLOOMSBURY

For Thomas and Georgina
and all the other children who have asked 'Where's Daddy?'

## Acknowledgements

All the women and men who completed questionnaires and
those who allowed us to interview them at great length.

John Curtis for reading the manuscript
and for his suggestions.

First published 1996 by Bloomsbury publishing Plc,
2 Soho Square, London W1V 6HB

A copy of the CIP entry for this book is available from
the British Library

ISBN 0 7475 2181 6

10 9 8 7 6 5 4 3 2 1

Designed by Hugh Adams
Typeset by Hewer Text Composition Services,
Edinburgh
Printed by Cox & Wyman Ltd, Reading Berkshire

'What of soul was left, I wonder, when the kissing had to stop?'

ROBERT BROWNING

# Statistics

|                                      | *1991*   | *1992*   | *1993*   |
| ------------------------------------ | -------- | -------- | -------- |
| DIVORCES                             | 158,745  | 160,385  | 165,018  |
| CHILDREN INVOLVED                    | 160,684  | 168,248  | 175,961  |
| DIVORCING COUPLES WITH CHILDREN      | 88,364   | 91,425   | 94,915   |

NUMBER OF DIVORCING COUPLES WITH:

|                          | *1991*  | *1992*  | *1993*  |
| ------------------------ | ------- | ------- | ------- |
| 1 CHILD                  | 35,663  | 36,225  | 36,911  |
| 2 CHILDREN               | 37,388  | 38,549  | 40,385  |
| 3 CHILDREN               | 11,816  | 12,735  | 13,767  |
| 4 CHILDREN               | 2,775   | 3,103   | 3,351   |
| 5 CHILDREN (or more)     | 704     | 813     | 901     |

[Statistics supplied by the Census Office, only available up to the end of 1993.]

Nine out of ten lone parents are mothers.

[Gingerbread]

# *Contents*

# CONTENTS

# Introduction

FIVE YEARS AGO, our family joined the ranks of the statistics that show that one in three (moving towards one in two) marriages end in divorce. Britain has the highest divorce rate in Europe. If present trends continue, one in four children will experience breakdown in their parents' marriage by the age of 16.

*Where's Daddy?* is neither a textbook nor a step-by-step guide to family breakup. The task of this book is to show families alternative ways to answer children's questions concerning separation and divorce and to provide some forewarning about the questions that will be asked.

In writing this book Jill has drawn from her work as a psychoanalytic psychotherapist and her understanding as a mother, grandmother, mother-in-law and, after 39 years of happy marriage, wife. Virginia, also a mother, speaks from her own recent experience of divorce. Together, as mother and grandmother, we had to find answers to many searching questions from Virginia's children, so have been able to draw on a wealth of personal experience.

We devised a questionnaire and from the replies we received, together with letters and the results of interviews, it seemed to us that the voices we heard spoke more eloquently than our own words. Therefore, we decided to let significant points emerge largely from the women and men telling their own stories. We also hear from the children through their writings and drawings.

We are very grateful to the vast number of women and men who gave us their time to share thoughts and feelings, not only

1

about their own painful situations, but about being a parent throughout the break-up of their family. The hindsight of one is of great value to the other. We must stress that all names and identifying features have been changed to maintain confidentiality.

We acknowledge that in most separations both partners have contributed – either consciously or unconsciously – to the break-up. Each has played a part. We are not here to judge, only to look at the different ways of helping the children. We remind ourselves that what spurred us to write *Where's Daddy?* was that we found ourselves having to answer the children's questions in a way that would be helpful to them and appropriate for their age.

When our family was going through the pain of a divorce, we would have appreciated the opportunity to read about other people's experiences. We would have been interested in the kind of questions their children asked, and in the different ways these questions were handled. Of course, there is no one right way – no blueprint – but it is some comfort to believe that others have been down these roads before. Every family is different and every situation is unique but there are lessons to be learnt from others. Some people were generous enough to tell us about errors they made in the hope that others could avoid similar pitfalls.

For the sake of clarity, the terms wife/husband is used although we acknowledge that other categories of couples with children separate. We speak of 'children' but also pay heed to the special needs of an only child. In addition, we also acknowledge that there are different reasons for the break-up of a family, although our book is particularly directed towards the family split by divorce. We realise that *Where's Daddy?* needs to be answered by parents who are bereaved, or who have to explain to children a parent's desertion or imprisonment.

*Where's Daddy?* could also have been called *Where's Mummy?*. We chose the former title because in our society it is still most likely to be the father who leaves and the mother who has the difficult questions to answer. According to Gingerbread (the organisation dedicated to helping one-parent families), nine out of ten lone parents are mothers. We hope, however, that a father on his own reading this book will find it helpful too. Much pain and suffering surrounds every separation and divorce. Something that seems to be such a private matter between two people soon bursts upon the extended family and friends and, in most cases, professionals such as solicitors, estate agents and other advisors. The 'fall out' is often unexpected, but always considerable, especially when there are children involved. Legally, divorce is now more straightforward, but the emotional side to divorce takes a very long time. Repeatedly, we were told, 'it hurt, it still hurts'.

While considering the effect that a separation of parents has upon the children, the same questions were asked time and again: 'What shall we tell the children?' and, most heart-breakingly, 'Where's Daddy?', 'Why has he gone?' and 'Doesn't he love me any more?'

In the following chapters we explore these questions, and others, and look at the different ways in which a parent might help their child with their emotions and their understanding of the family situation. Adults should not assume that a child has correctly understood a situation, and perceptions will vary according to age and intelligence. There is no right way, and no easy way, to tell a child that something is happening that will change their life for ever. Always remember that each family situation is unique.

In our research for this book, we were in contact with many parents, from those on the brink of separation to others divorced for many years. We learned from adults who can remember what they were, or were not, told when their parents separated and of the effect upon them throughout their lives. Also, we were told by some what it is like to ask, 'Where's Daddy?'

Being overwhelmed by loss is something that all the lone parents mentioned, and in many cases this was compounded by financial worries, but loss of self-esteem and of friends and family was also apparent.

It is in the middle of the crisis of separation, when feeling most vulnerable, that thought has to be given to the children. Children also need to be updated as the situation evolves.

By reading our book we hope you will be helped to find the best way for you and your family to get through a painful situation and perhaps to be a little clearer about, 'What shall we tell the children?'

Jill Curtis
Virginia Ellis

# Chapter 1
# *The Beginning of the End*

---

> '*Time present and time past are both perhaps present in time future.*'
>
> T.S. ELIOT

> '*You never really know a man until you have divorced him.*'
>
> ZSA ZSA GABOR

BEFORE THERE is a divorce there has to be a wedding and we looked closely at the early days of a relationship.

All the world loves a bride – heads turn in the street at the sight of a bridal car and women's magazines have long learnt that to put a photograph of a bride on the cover boosts sales. From the moment the idea of a wedding is mooted, the family are bombarded by information on how to do this, that and the other. There are guides on how to be a best man, groom and mother-in-law, and no shortage of detailed instructions about how many bridesmaids and cars are needed and where to get the cake. In every newsagent's there are magazines specifically for women thinking of a wedding – etiquette is there for all to behold. It is a time for everyone to celebrate.

On the other hand, women in the no-man's land of separation are thrust into the position of trying to deal with one of the most painful and traumatic times of their life, without the benefit of a map or even of any sign posts. Add to that the extra dimension of trying to explain to the children of the relationship just what is happening, when perhaps not clear oneself, and one can be left floundering and lost.

*'Each time I looked at Mary playing and happy, my eyes filled with tears; how could I tell her that the bottom had dropped out of my world and was about to drop out of hers? Nothing would ever be the same again, and that's a fact.'*

Lucy (one daughter, Mary, age 3)

What is often difficult for the outsider to see is that even if the relationship has been quite obviously and openly going through a hard time, the actual shock and fear when the break in the marriage comes is none the less real and painful. It can be hard when caring friends and relations say, 'You're better off without him.' This may be true in the long run, and perhaps you know that, but at first it isn't what you want to hear. Nor is it helpful to be told, 'I never liked him, I always thought he was odd/bad tempered/had a roving eye.' However much you have been hurt by your partner, it is hard to think that family and friends have been harbouring these thoughts. After all, he is the man you married and shared your life with and he is the father of your children. There may be some relief that an unhappy marriage is over but almost certainly love was there when you set out together, and because of this you will feel loss.

## EARLY WARNING SIGNS

But let's start at the beginning. We were surprised to be told by so many women that they sensed some unease within themselves either around the time of their marriage or shortly afterwards. Most put it down to 'wedding nerves' or 'the honeymoon being over'. Can it be that even in the 1990s there is still pressure on women, even if felt unconsciously, to marry and 'live happily ever after'?

*'I remember quite clearly thinking on my honeymoon that I'd made a mistake, but by the time we came home I was pregnant, so just got on with life. Seven years later when Ben walked out on us, I remembered my doubts. I think I had just wallpapered over them and got on with having kids.'*

Jean

*'I thought that having a baby would cement Tom and me together as a couple, it took five years for Tom to leave.'*

Mary

He shocked her by saying that he had never wanted children but she'd never listened to him. Mary said when faced by her two children (ten and eight) asking, 'what's happened?', she felt if she was honest that 'what happened' had happened eleven years earlier.

Here we have two examples of women not listening to their own feelings and failing to act on them.

Jean went on to tell us:

*'I had so little self-esteem that I couldn't imagine anyone else wanting to marry me, so jumped at the chance to marry Ben even though I "knew" the match wasn't right. My parents had divorced when I was an adolescent and I felt, looking back, I had been desperate to create a new home and family. When Ben left me I had to face a breakdown of family life for the second time and this time I had a six-year-old son to care for too.'*

Jean

*'I was thinking the other night about what had attracted me to Pete in the first place. He was confident, popular, fun loving, generous and had kind green eyes. When I think of the past 15 years, I see him unable to hold on and develop any real relationships — knowing hundreds of people but very few true friends. He is extravagant and reckless with money, selfish and a liar.'*

Marjorie

It seemed to us that although Marjorie could move from romantic love to a mature relationship, Pete was unable to do this. Marjorie told us that after leaving her, Pete had a succession of affairs. 'Falling in love' held an adolescent attraction for Pete; holding on to a relationship was another matter. This was similar to Julie's story.

*'When I think about my marriage and what went wrong I think that basically I outgrew my husband and what we had together. On meeting him I was unconfident in my first full-time job, shy with new people and had just finished a four-year relationship that was going nowhere near the altar. During the years of marriage I became more confident, a stronger person, more sure of my chosen career and later, through becoming a mother, happier with my own feelings and ideas. Over the years my husband didn't like my new-found confidence and shied away from me. What made the situation worse was Jerry then lost his job and the one he took in desperation seven months later he felt was beneath him. Our relationship carried on deteriorating over the next few years until he moved in with the 17-year-old typist who made him feel like a king.'*

Julie

It is true that we can blind ourselves so that we do not see what we don't want to see.

*'I realise now that I never trusted him. I always thought there was another side of him I wasn't part of. So nothing has changed, except we are divorced.'*

Shelly

*'I know what Shelly means. I'm crying now not because I can't have more, but because the little we share now is practically all we ever had.'*

Liza

Jean described clearly something we heard again and again – ignoring signs that there were problems in the relationship.

*'Of course, with hindsight, all the signs were there that our marriage was failing but I wouldn't – I couldn't – let myself believe it. Ben was coming home later and later, and even then I told myself he was working hard and I shouldn't make a fuss. Often the excuses he made didn't hold water, but I stopped myself thinking things through. The day he told me he was leaving was*

8

*like being struck by a thunderbolt. I told him I had no idea there was anything going on and I think he found that hard to believe. Only much later could I admit even to myself that I had known, deep inside, that he was seeing someone else.'*

Jean

*'My husband started going into the office at ten o'clock at night. I didn't question it for a long time – then I got suspicious.'*

Karen

The difficulty is facing up to the fact that perhaps the marriage was not made in heaven and that something is terribly wrong. So many women feel that if they keep their heads down and hold on tight, whatever is threatening their marriage will go away.

# LEADING UP TO A SEPARATION
This period, we were frequently told, can be a nightmare.

*'Did we talk? Well, I spoke for two and didn't listen because I didn't like what I was hearing.'*

Heather

*'One Sunday evening I had just handed my husband his supper on a plate, when he said to me "I don't want to be married any more, I want some time alone". I could not answer him, so went on eating. He said – sounding very relieved – "You are taking this so well."*

Colette

*'We were driving away from a village one evening after a meal out when my husband said, "That was a nice place, I think I might come and live here". I asked, uncomprehendingly, "What are you talking about?" and he replied, "I need some space and want to live alone now."*

Angie

*'I shudder at the memory of the time before we broke up. I couldn't enjoy being with the children or even cope with them.*

*I stayed hidden in my room and left them to be looked after by the au pair.'*

Christine

Later, Christine told us that the best thing that has come from the divorce is the new strong relationship she has with her son and daughter.

*'Family life? We didn't have one for about two years before we split up.'*

Marie

*'I trembled at the thought of being on my own if we broke up, but I did know something dramatic had to change.'*

Leonie

*'We were OK together in the first years, but after the children were born, we never, ever, agreed on any matter especially relating to childcare. When do you know if things are bad enough to say, enough, or for him to say it?'*

Connie

After all, the thinking goes, you are a couple and recognised as that by family, friends and neighbours – how could things really disintegrate? At the end of the day, how could he leave, you are a family, you have children and he couldn't really go . . . or could he?

The women who shared their experiences with us spoke of husbands who, before leaving, did indicate in many ways that the relationship was on the rocks. Some laughed, some cried as they told us how gullible they must have seemed to their husbands as they appeared to swallow tales of missed planes, motorway holdups and extended conferences.

*'I couldn't really believe that my steady reliable husband had suddenly begun to have all these misfortunes – it was only when a hotel rang to ask if my husband or myself had by mistake removed*

*the remote control from our hotel room the previous night, that I knew I could no longer pretend even to myself that he was not involved with someone else. When I confronted David with this I think that initially we were both relieved that everything was finally in the open. The feeling of relief soon faded into despair as the reality struck home and I thought of the children and what we would tell them.'*

Jenny

*'We were OK as a family and then Derek was made redundant; it had a terrible effect on him. Then he started to stay out all night. This was so out of character. We'd been together for 15 years and had three kids. I was sick with worry and lost a lot of weight. The children became very worried too, they soon picked up something was wrong, and things went from bad to worse.'*

Nicola

*'The children noticed I was very upset, because my husband's behaviour to me was so startlingly different from what it had always been. They began to ask questions I didn't dare ask like, "Why is Daddy being horrible – doesn't he love you any more?"'*

Louise

There are some friendly divorces and on one level this must be reassuring for everyone concerned. However, it can be perplexing for the children trying to understand the need for divorce. In addition the hope for a fully reunited family is kept in front of the children, but out of reach. There are still questions to be answered and explanations, appropriate to the children's ages, to be made.

## THE EFFECT ON FRIENDS AND FAMILY

When a couple are possibly on the brink of separation, it is also a difficult period for friends and family. At times the couple might – separately – talk to the same person, giving their version of what is happening. The urge to be a peacemaker can be strong, but it is easy to get your fingers burned trying to play this part. This can be a very uncomfortable place to be. If there is a reconciliation close friends and family can – to their surprise – find themselves cast as troublemakers.

*'My daughter Jean found out that my son-in-law was having an affair. She came crying to me and the whole family rallied around her. For nearly a year we supported her, not only emotionally, but financially too. Then, just like that, David said he was coming back home. The first we knew of it was when one of the children told me. Jean became very frosty towards all of us – it was as if we had done something. It nearly broke my heart – I hardly see the children now; it's as if Jean and I have had a divorce.'*

Jess

Divorces used to happen to 'other' people, in 'other' families. Not so long ago a proud boast used to be, 'there has never been a divorce in our family'. Divorces were for Hollywood film stars. Alas, now that is not so and the spectre of divorce – no longer a social disgrace – has crept over us all in one way or another. However, because it is more common, it does not mean that it is less traumatic for all involved.

*'I married into a Jewish family – I converted and I thought that showed my commitment and love for my husband and his family. One week before our wedding my future father-in-law took me to one side and said, "You do know that in our eyes there is no divorce, if you marry, you marry. There is no way out, only death." He illustrated his point by talking about the family. He was right – in a family of some 50 couples there were no divorces in any generation. I can only be relieved that he did not live to see two of his sons divorced, and one of his brothers. He would have found the changes incomprehensible and totally unacceptable.'*

Rebecca

*'My dad went to see my husband and urged him to reconsider – this wasn't because of me, I think, but because the children were still very small. He refused.'*

Sarah

We met May, mother of Jane and grandmother of Lucy (4½) and Olivia (3).

'When Jane told me she and Hugh were separating, I thought I would die. I know times change, but in my day you just got on with marriage. I still think it is too easy for these young people just to give up. I told Jane this.'

May

'What my mother found so hard to understand is that I had no choice. Hugh just told me that he'd had enough of being married and wanted to be free to live his life the way he wanted. I begged him to stay if not for my sake, for Lucy and Olivia. It was the last straw when my mother told me to try harder.'

Jane

'I still think you did not handle Hugh properly – you young women think you know it all. Perhaps you shouldn't have expected so much from Hugh. You certainly expected him to help a lot when Lucy was born, you know.'

May

'Of course I did! We decided together to have two babies close in age – of course I expected him to help.'

Jane

'When you and your sister were small, you were both in bed when your father came home. I didn't expect him to be running around changing nappies. I still think you made a mistake telling everybody that Hugh wanted to go. If you had taken my advice, you would have kept quiet and it would all have blown over.'

May

'Mother, Hugh had left me. He wasn't living with us and he certainly had no intention of coming back: how could I not tell you and my friends about the trouble I was in? I needed help – the children needed help.'

Jane

Jane and May began to cry together. The pain of their very recent experience was clear. Jane had lost a partner and a full-time father for her children, but May too had lost the idea of a happily married daughter and a secure family unit for her granddaughters to grow up in. May went on to tell us that she felt she had also lost a much-loved son in Hugh and found this very hard to accept.

*'He never even said goodbye to me.'*

May

May wept. As Jane listened to her mother the full force of the pain the extended family were feeling overwhelmed her, but she began to understand that her mother's apparent brusqueness was in fact covering up a multitude of feelings.

Those of us untouched by a divorce in the family may find it difficult to believe the knock-on effect that such news has on a close extended family.

*'I'll never forget the look of despair on my mother's face – there was real pain – when I told her Jim had left us. Her eyes filled with tears, and I hadn't bargained on that.'*

Pat

Other women told us of the reactions of brothers, sisters and grandparents, too.

*'The worst thing was telling my grandparents, both in their 80s and very frail. They both cried, and my grandfather said he felt so helpless.'*

Dee

*'When my sister was divorced I helped her with her children. Then I found my children were sad and puzzled too. I hadn't thought at first of the effect on them, and the shock they must have felt when their uncle left – they learnt a hard way that "daddies" can go away. I had to find answers for them too.'*

Sarah

*'It brought it home to me when I started telling friends about the separation. If they had children they often said, "Do you really know what you're doing?" It made me feel even worse than I already did.'*

Henry

*'Family and friends feel depressed for you especially if they are married, and you feel their concern for the children. It's a case of there but for the grace of God, I suppose. I felt a terrible admission of failing, and its all those lost dreams I guess.'*

Beryl

*'I could not tell my mother about the problems I was having in my marriage. She had just had terminal cancer diagnosed and for nine months I visited her "cheerfully" whilst howling to myself to and from the hospital. The loss of my husband and mother coming simultaneously was too much to bear. Not only that, but I was frantic about what to tell the children when I knew two important figures in their lives were disappearing.'*

Emily

## CAN THEY HELP?

We were sad to learn that although some families rallied around, others were not so sympathetic or supportive. Blame and accusations flew through the air and frequently the advice was, 'don't separate, think of the children'. 'As if I was thinking of anyone else,' Jane said.

The advice, 'don't do it', in fact seemed to encourage many women to stick it out longer and to try to ignore the growing signs around them.

*'I was very unhappy and Bill was hardly ever at home. When he was, we didn't speak and looking back that can't have been a good atmosphere for Mary to grow up in. I was nearly always in tears and when one day Mary put her little arms round me and said "Don't worry, Mummy, I'll cheer you up" I knew I had to do something. It wasn't right that a 3-year-old should be mothering me. I spoke to*

*Bill that night and brought things to a head. My family still think I was wrong to do this and we should have stayed together for Mary's sake. But after that day in the garden I knew I had to take control of my life again and look after Mary. I realised that it was the uncertainty of the situation which was so terrible. Bill and I did split up, but we began talking again and together we could talk about how and what to tell Mary. Before I could do that, I had to stop crying so much, and so did Bill.'*

Lucy

*'Everyone was so shocked to hear about us; they thought we were an ideal couple. A loving family. My friends envied all we had. They wanted to give him a kick up the backside.'*

Jackie

Many women find women friends (and sometimes men friends) to talk to, but many talked about some who were – at the beginning – very keen to listen and to know every detail of the drama as it unfolded.

*'I felt very let down by some of my girlfriends. It is true that I did need to talk a lot at the beginning and some friends were good – but most of them seemed to like the gossip side of it all. They would shriek, "He didn't" and "What did you say then?" They were eager to know the details. As time went on though they lost interest – but to be fair I suppose they just began to get on with their lives and got a bit fed-up with me and my situation which did go on and on. I was very undecided about whether or not to leave Donald; after all Harry was only a baby. I wished I hadn't told my friends some of the details because they would often try to influence me to do something one way or another. Poor Donald had to run the gauntlet of the women's neighbourhood mafia and that didn't help our relationship at home, I can tell you.'*

Amanda

We were told also of friends' awkwardness – of their not knowing whether to say, 'good riddance' or 'I'm sorry' – so in the end many said nothing.

If there is a reconciliation or an attempt to 'try again', what happens to all the personal details that have been spilled out in the heat of the moment to family and friends? Louise certainly blames her family for making the break-up finally happen.

*'Matt and I did try to make a go of it and he left his girlfriend and came back to us just before Christmas. We went to my parents on Christmas Day and my father didn't speak to him, Mum looked daggers and my brother kept making not-very-funny jokes about "absent friends" and "bits on the side". It was probably the unhappiest day of my life. When we got home Matt and I had the worst row ever and Matt accused me of washing our linen in public – but he had had his girlfriend to talk to; I had to talk things over with Mum and Dad.'*

Louise

Part of the need to talk over the situation again and again is actually an effort to try to understand it oneself. Louise, after her husband left, spent many hours going round the house crying and saying 'why?' over and over again.

*'I had this urge to talk, talk, talk. I couldn't tire of it. We all felt the same, my separated friends and I, we found we just had to talk over such little details that anyone not having been through the same experiences would think so trivial and petty.'*

Louise

*'I almost needed to talk it away, as if I needed to say the words, "He has left me", before they could be cleansed and I'd be free of the awful pain. It was as if talking about it gave it the importance it deserved and then, and only then, could it be forgotten. It reminded me of writing a diary which became an obsession for me in my teens.'*

Amanda

# BANDING TOGETHER

Certainly, women found comfort in getting together to compare notes. Often they were able to feel anger more easily on behalf of each other's situation.

> 'When my husband first went I was in shock for months to the extent that I couldn't feel angry at all and I would listen uncomprehendingly to friends and family getting so het up on my behalf over what happened.'
>
> Jessie

It would seem that, at times, it was close family and friends who 'carried' the anger and experienced it more directly than the women concerned.

> 'I couldn't understand why Jennifer was so tearful but not furious enough. I admired Sarah Graham Moon who cut the arms off her husband's suits when she discovered he had betrayed her.'
>
> Jennifers's mother

This alludes to a well publicised event when Lady Sarah Graham Moon did just that to the admiration and applause of many, becoming celebrated by the media for her actions. Perhaps the reason why so many people's imaginations were caught by Sarah Moon's story was because she put into action the kind of things that most women only dream of doing. When she leapt out of her car with scissors in hand her errant husband was so astonished he fell over backwards into a flowerbed. Sarah Moon's distribution of her husband's treasured wine around the village brought tears of joy to many women, and perhaps tears of another kind to many anxious men!

The grapevine soon links up women in a similar position and women who did band together found strength and support. They would ponder and struggle over issues and questions of what to say or do. Even informal chats outside school gates were felt to be helpful and often comforting. It is very hard to struggle alone to make important decisions.

*'We would frequently be very brave on behalf of one of our group. The room would ring with instructions: "You tell him . . ." or, "Don't let him get away with that . . ." The truth is we were often not so brave when it came to a meeting with our own ex!'*

Jennifer

However, they did seem to spur each other to keep on going. Irene, who was more isolated, found it hard to do just that.

*'I had no family to turn to and I must tell you I became so depressed I thought of killing myself and Alex. There is no word for the feeling of total inner pain that you think can't get any worse and then you are hit with a new trauma, new problems. At times the only saying which came to mind was "to kick a dog when he's down". I'll never know how I did survive. I just clung on to Alex, really.'*

Irene (mother of Alex, 6 months)

A health visitor proved to be a friend indeed, and encouraged Irene to see the counsellor attached to her GP practice (the different forms of professional help available are discussed more fully in Chapter 6).

*'It did help. I found myself looking forward to our time each week. I could let off steam or cry, and know that it was my time and I could say what I needed to without worrying if I was boring her or upsetting her. Yes, the counsellor helped me and in turn helped Alex, I suppose. I shudder to think where we would have been now if I hadn't followed my health visitor's advice.'*

Irene

Women can become very socially isolated after the separation.

*'I'd be asked to tea with the kids, but somehow invitations to dinner from couples we used to know certainly dried up.'*

Margaret

This was also felt to be common with some widows we spoke to. In our society many people are uncomfortable with grief or death and a divorce has features of both.

# THE BREAKING POINT

Perhaps there has been infidelity or violence in the marriage. Sometimes this has been overlooked or forgiven once or even many times, but then one day something happens that makes this impossible. All of us have a breaking point.

*'I always knew my husband had one-night stands when he was away on business trips. At first I used to cry and make a fuss, but I knew I'd never change him. Eventually, I stopped caring or so I thought, until one day my brother-in-law rang to say he'd discovered that my husband and my sister had been away for the night together. My brother-in-law was going to forgive my sister and to forget, he said, but for me that was not an option, it was the end. I took the children and left Fred. He could never understand why this time it was different, but it was because it was now open in the family and that was something I could not overlook. I had to draw the line. It split up the whole family of course.'*

Irene

*'Mike was violent towards me from time to time. After he had hit me he was always sorry, and it didn't happen that often; he just lost his temper, like his dad did. He never touched the kids though. One day on our way back home the kids started fighting in the back of the car. I could see Mike was getting steamed up, Billy was rude once too often and Mike turned round and hit him full on the face. That night I began to think in a way I hadn't before. It was one thing Mike having a go at me – but quite another if he was going to start on his kids – our Billy was only 11 at the time. I went to a counsellor to try to work out with her why I had put up with so much anger and aggression from Mike. Once I understood the unconscious reasons for this I could mobilise my anger in a constructive way and began a train of events which ended in our divorce. In a way that was the easy part – the difficult part was telling the children. The two eldest loved their father, and it was only Billy who, like me, got the rough side of Mike. Billy could understand why I was breaking up the family, but Jim and Robert could not. They seemed to think that if Billy and I "behaved" we*

*could be a happy family. I knew it was more than that, and even*
*though he was so young, so did Billy.'*

Pat

So for Pat, her children were brought into the discussion early
on and they had plenty to say. For Billy the way was clear, but Jim
and Robert had very divided loyalties. They witnessed the
increasing violence in the family as they saw their mother making
more of a stand. To the older children this often seemed to be
making the situation worse and, partly through fear, they would
freeze into silence and accuse Pat and Billy of making trouble.
Much later on, Robert told his mother that he was silent for fear his
Dad would turn his attention away from Billy on to him. Because
Pat's children were older, she accepted from the start that they
should be involved. When children are younger it is easier to
think and to hope that they don't understand what is going on.

*'My husband and I were on the motorway with the children in the*
*back. We were having a dreadful row and swearing at each other.*
*What we didn't realise was that Martin was speeding and a police*
*car was behind us. It suddenly flashed the car and pulled us over.*
*The policeman cautioned Martin about the speed he was driving at,*
*but also said we should pay more attention to the road as he had*
*seen us rowing. As we drove off it made me question for the first time*
*what effect this scare might have had on Linda and Matilda. After*
*all they had been sitting there watching and that must have been*
*very frightening for them. I pondered for some time about what they*
*would have made of it, and whether I should say something to them.*
*But I didn't know what to say and convinced myself they were too*
*young to understand or to notice. I was wrong, very wrong. Only*
*later did I see the effect on them both – they became very timid,*
*withdrawn children.'*

Sara (mother of two daughters aged 4 and 2½)

*'My children saw their daddy punch me in the face – they weren't*
*sure what was going on until I explained that Daddy was naughty.*
*My friends told me to leave him, but I wasn't sure that was best for*

*us all. I had to leave in my own time and that meant two more years of violence. My friends lost patience with me, but I had to make my preparations and be sure.'*

Maggie

*'"Stand by your man," sings Tammy Wynett. I didn't have a chance to do that. He was just up and off and left me to tell the children. I thought he was trying to build up a business, working late and at weekends. What he was doing was trying to build up his self-esteem with a string of affairs.'*

Sue

This was a thread that linked many of the women who spoke to us, especially in cases of adultery. We were told again and again that women felt they had no chance to repair the relationship. Decisions were already made that would affect many lives before they were even told.

*'The children learned about the separation when they witnessed it as I did, in disbelief, at the point of departure.'*

Susan

# CONCLUSIONS

It is a bonus when friends and family are there to offer support and advice even if their reactions are not always the expected ones. We can now understand more about the difficulties of when and what to tell close friends and family and the effect of the news upon them. As difficult as this can be, in the next chapter we explore the even harder task of telling the children.

# Chapter 2
# *The Questions Children Ask*

'Of all the hatred the world produces, a wife's hatred
for her husband, when she does hate him, is the
strongest.'

ANTHONY TROLLOPE

## DO CHILDREN PICK UP CLUES?

Worrying about what the children sense and what they understand is one of the main concerns of parents on the brink of
separation.

At what age are children aware of 'grown-up' problems,
especially between their parents? Gloria could not believe that
a one-year-old could sense that something was wrong. If you have
ever been on holiday in a country where you do not speak the
language, however, you almost certainly had no difficulty in
knowing when a taxi driver was furiously demanding a bigger
tip or in responding equally quickly to the warm and welcoming
attitude of a hotel receptionist. Reluctantly, Gloria added that only
last night she had turned on the television to find a French film
half way through.

> 'I can't speak French but after five minutes I could pick up the
> atmosphere and the tension and know it was a chiller. I suppose it
> must be just like a small child unable to understand the words, but
> still picking up what is in the air.'

Gloria

Some people were able to pinpoint specific times and occasions when what was happening to the family became a matter for discussion or debate. Others were not so sure and hoped that it was a gradual dawning and understanding of change.

*'I talked a lot on the 'phone and the boys invariably listened in. In a way it helped them understand what had been going on without asking direct questions.'*

Debbie

*'When did the children first pick up that something was wrong? I'm not sure exactly, but the moment it was obvious was when we were on holiday in Venice. We were sightseeing in the Doge's Palace – the children were very excited, as I was. As we climbed first the staircase of the Giants and then the Golden Staircase I heard Samuel say to Sally, "Look at Mum looking up at the wonderful decoration on the ceiling as we climb, and Dad is grumbling about all these stairs." Something about the tone in his voice made me stop. He was right and that comment summed up the state of our relationship. We no longer looked in the same direction – I had felt that for a long time, and now Samuel had picked it up and clicked it into place. That night Alan and I had a talk and he told me he was very unhappy and wanted to leave us, but didn't know how to. I guess you could say Venice is where we finally knew we had fallen out of love. Sad, really.'*

Faith (mother of Samuel and Sally)

*'The children were with me when I clicked that something was odd, very odd. We got in my husband's car and I found a well-thumbed guide to country house hotels. Well, I'd never been to one and I said, more or less as a joke, "Is this where you take her?" The look on my husband's face said it all and I burst into tears. Then, as on cue, so did both the children. We must have looked a sorry sight because then my husband started to cry too. The children were very young then – 5 and 7 – but they still remember that time and call it "the day we all boo-hoo'd". Looking back, I suppose I did already have an inkling, perhaps an unconscious one, otherwise why did I*

*phrase my question like that? I do wish the kids hadn't been there, though, and I know my husband – my ex-husband – does too. I wasn't able to answer any of their questions then, although I did later. There was plenty of time – years in fact – when we all asked, and answered, each other's questions. One fell swoop for us all I'm afraid.'*

Pauline

*'How did I find out about my husband's affair? My husband and I were going through a bad patch. He was saying he wanted "more space for himself". We agreed I should go away with the children and my parents for three weeks to the seaside, and he would have time "to think". Half way through the holiday I had the urge to go home unexpectedly. I did, and found he had moved his mistress into our house. I took a long time to recover from that – the marriage of course did not recover.'*

Anna

*'I truly thought we were a happy family. George was going on a business trip and I took him to the airport. The children came too. I dropped him off and we waved goodbye – kisses all round. Then the boys begged me to park and let them see their father off and to watch the planes. We wandered back into the departure hall and saw George with his arm round my best friend. We all stood and looked at each other. George was, and still is, a loving father and the boys adore him. We are divorced now, but from the start I concentrated on telling the boys that the divorce was a grown-up thing. George and I were divorcing; the children weren't. They still had a mother and a father who loved them and they could have us separately but not together. I was the one who didn't have a husband or a best friend, but infidelity should be no concern of the children.'*

Gloria

For Gloria and her children the situation was immediate and they were all thrust into the line of fire in a single moment. When George left, the children knew where their father was and they also knew why he had gone.

*'There were some initial problems. Our eldest boy did not want to visit him but I was always quite firm. Graham asked why he had to see his father and I would reply, "because he is your father and you need him". Graham might not know it now but a boy does need his father and it was up to me to see the contact was maintained right from the start. I know years from now Graham will appreciate what I have done.'*

Gloria

Gloria seems to have been able to look at events in a cool and unemotional way, at least for some of the time, but it is not always possible to do this. As she says, everything was there on a plate for them all to see, no secrets – but surely not without pain?

We heard about children picking up the problems in their parents' relationship in so many different ways, and often we saw what a large part the unconscious played in bringing troubles to the surface.

*'We all found out in the most extraordinary way. One evening my four-year-old had a nightmare – both my husband and I got up and went to his room but it was an uphill task to comfort him. In order to pacify him I asked what he had been dreaming and through sobs he said, "Daddy is going away and not taking us." I turned to look at my husband for him to speak to Edward but he was overcome with emotion. I don't know how I got Edward back to sleep but, once I did, Phil and I had a long night ahead when he admitted he was having a relationship with his secretary and didn't know what to do or how to tell me. He was as shocked as I when Edward did it for him.'*

Hester

When asked 'How did the children learn about the separation?' Angela replied:

*'My children learnt when we fled the home. They knew we were in danger. The children had witnessed arguments and saw me bruised. You cannot reason with a violent drunk. It was live or die for me.'*

Angela

*'They saw me cry far too much, lose three stone in weight and saw me bruised, emotionally and physically.'*

Petal

*'I think my children picked up that things weren't right before I did. My son, aged 5, was bedwetting, overactive and biting his lip. He'd had nightmares before the separation. My daughter was clingy and unconfident and even at 9 years old was unable to stay a night away from home. She became very dependent on me, but was close to her father and very shocked by our separation when it happened.'*

Clare

Clare went on to tell us that she focused her attention on the children but deeply regrets that she didn't understand their distress and failed to see that they were picking up the pain in the home. She took her son to a child psychotherapist; he was greatly helped and continued to see the therapist for three years. During this time the reason for the eventual divorce came to light, as the whole family were told of the other women in their father's life. The reasons for the break-up were a secret from the children and from Clare for several years before this. The children were picking up on an unconscious level that their security was in jeopardy and reacting to this.

Carol said that she felt sad when replying to our question, 'At what point did the children first pick up that things were not right?'

*'The children did not pick up signs because there was no love in the marriage and it had always been that way, even when the children were born, and so they knew no better.'*

Carol

Olive said she felt like Carol and that 'things had never been "right" so the children had no idea that "right" would have been different from their experience – they suffered anxiety when their father threw plates at the tea table, but perhaps they thought all fathers did that . . .'

Although our main task is to find answers to children's questions, naturally we also learn from listening to what the children themselves have to say. We can gain understanding and insight from their clear vision but we do not always hear what they tell us.

*'My daughter was nearly 4 when Neil left us. She believed in Father Christmas at the time. I only realised how much she missed her dad when she said, wistfully, "Perhaps one night Daddy will come down the chimney to visit me." I got on the phone to Neil at once and said that he had to see her regularly. Up to that point I'm afraid we had both thought about ourselves and had assumed she didn't notice much about what was going on. We had thought she was too little to have an opinion about whether or not she saw her dad, and I don't think Neil cared whether he saw her again.'*

Evelyn

# CHILDREN BEGIN TO ASK QUESTIONS

It can be a relief to realise that the same questions come again and again in many guises, giving parents the opportunity to have a second or third chance at answering them in a clear and less confused way.

Children go on asking questions, often repeating them in different ways. They need to know what is happening to them and to their lives. They often probe at awkward and inconvenient times and they go on asking. What satisfies one child at one time in his or her life will not pacify another. There is a thirst to know and this is sometimes hard to quench when the questions are asked in an oblique way or perhaps signalled by bad behaviour or a psychosomatic symptom. An irritating cough, possibly years after the break-up, can herald the arrival of yet another phase in the questioning, and questions and answers need to be explored. As the questions change, so the answers will have to be updated. As time goes by, the way you look back at events will also have changed and this will be reflected in your replies.

Some questions seem to have been asked by all the children. If there are major changes at home and the father leaves the family for whatever reason, there will be questions. If not asked out loud, they will be in the child's mind. One source of anxiety and questions will be the fear that it is their fault: 'Did I make him go?', 'Was it something I did or didn't do?'

Questions were often direct: Pauline told us that her 11-year-old son asked: 'Where does Daddy stay?', 'Why doesn't Daddy come home?', 'Is he working?', 'Is he up the pub again?', 'Why do you love him?' and 'Why hasn't he given you any money?' She told us that she answered these questions honestly and simply but that it didn't make it any easier.

*'My daughter asked me if we split up what would be the arrangements, and would she have a say in them.'*

Susie

*'All of a sudden questions came thick and fast. Why doesn't Daddy come home? Won't you let him?'*

Barbara

To answer 'Why has he gone?' can be very complicated.

*'My son asked my mum and she told him that his dad had got fed up and left us all. Later, I heard that he asked my friend who told him his dad must have gone mad. By the time he asked me he was very confused. I could only tell Timmy the truth that nobody knew why.'*

Sharon

*'My 13-year-old daughter kept asking me if Daddy had left because of something she did, or something I did or didn't do. I told her that she was not to blame and that it wasn't really anyone's fault. When she said over and over again that she wanted us both, I told her that it just sometimes doesn't work like that.'*

Sandra

*'I'll never forget the first time my daughter said the words I'd dreaded: "Why did Daddy go? Why did Daddy leave us?" I had*

*rehearsed in my head the answers I would give when she asked them. However, my mind went blank – how do you answer questions like that?'*

Gillian

Many women said that at a similar moment they felt very unprepared – and some women told us that they thought they either said too much or too little at that time.

*'If she had asked me when he first left I wouldn't have been able to contain my anger and I would have said much more than she needed to hear. Four years on when she did ask, I dithered because I didn't want to paint a completely biased picture of the man she spends a fair bit of time with. I waffled, I'm afraid.'*

Gillian

Flexibility and listening to what children are asking is important. Questions and answers will change as time goes by and the circumstances change. Also, your own feelings will not be so near the surface and therefore you can choose what it is appropriate to say and what should not be discussed in front of the children.

Whatever the age of the child or children of the family, the repercussions are often dramatic and are long-lasting.

*'My son began to ask questions right from the start. The questions continue today in many different ways and on many different levels.'*

Pippa

We will consider the effects of separation on grown-up children later (Chapter 5).

# 'DOESN'T DADDY LOVE ME ANY MORE?'

Careful handling is needed when children ask mothers about fathers, especially if they have no contact with them: 'Doesn't Daddy love me any more?' Some mothers say, 'of course he does', whereas others do not feel it is wise or in the child's best interest to build a false picture of a failed relationship.

Hilda and Ann, both mothers on their own with a 5-year-old child, shared their experiences of dealing with the same question with each other and with us. Both fathers did visit their sons.

*'When James asked me this, my heart almost stopped beating, although I had been expecting the question. In fact I had rehearsed an answer. I felt my eyes fill with tears but I took him on my lap and said that although it must be hard for him to understand, because Daddy doesn't live with us now, his daddy does love him very much indeed.'*

Hilda

Ann exploded with rage when she heard this:

*'I told Tom right from the start, his daddy had chosen to go to a new family and it was his new family he loved now. Daddy wanted to live with his girlfriend and didn't want us any more.'*

Ann

Hilda looked uncomfortable as she listened and said to Ann:

*'I wonder if you really heard Tom's question. All he was asking was did his daddy still love him? I think you loaded too much onto him. He would have felt and heard your anger, and perhaps thought you were cross with him for even asking.'*

Hilda

*'I have to admit what you say makes sense. Of course his dad still loves him, even I can see that, and yet I didn't tell Tom that.'*

Ann

*'Sam asked me if his dad loved him but I side-stepped the question. I told my son, then 5, that we were going to leave home. I was pregnant with my daughter at the time but had decided to go once and for all. We went to live with a friend of mine who my son had met before, and we took the nanny. My son did have problems, but*

*he had them before we left, I think because of the way his father behaved towards him and treated me.'*

Claire

*'Don't worry too much about what to tell the children – just listen to them and what they are asking. The answers will generally just follow on.'*

Susan

Margaret did not find things at all straightforward:

*'Children will often ask questions that you are not able to answer or not ready to talk about, and what happens then?'*

Margaret

It is a hard fact that at a time when children most need parenting parents are often not in a state to be able to offer it. This is something children pick up – unconsciously – and they may try to protect their parents in the belief that they will only be another burden if they ask questions.

*'My son Edward would ask and answer his own questions. "Why don't we have enough money? Oh yes, Daddy now has two houses and more children to pay for."'*

Laura

*'Of course, children want to ask, "what is going to happen to us now that Daddy doesn't live here any more?" It's not easy to answer when you yourself are afraid of the future, but do be sure not to make your children feel bad for asking the questions.'*

Henrietta

*'Good advice from Henrietta, but it was hard for me to tolerate their questions when I felt so helpless. I wanted to shout at them, "I feel the same, and don't give me a hard time because its not my fault."'*

Fiona

Some questions are still asked years later:

*'My daughter, Sylvia, is 18 and needs to know if her father ever loved her. My husband left us when she was 2 years old and it is now that she is so upset and depressed. She has had her first boyfriend trouble and I think being left by him has activated a lot of other things. I found her crying over a photo of herself as a baby on my ex's shoulders. She says that she feels she has nothing inside her and what kind of person can she be if her father left her as a baby? She asked so many questions. Did we still love each other when she was conceived? Sylvia said that if she was not conceived from love it wiped out her whole existence. Her older sister says she feels OK but I think its because Audrey has more earlier memories of a family.'*

Susie

*'Vicky was only 14 when her father left and she started having real difficulties at school. Eventually, her behaviour was so bad that she had to be excluded from school. We got help from a child psychiatrist who helped to bring things to the surface. Her father had left us to live with Vicky's best friend's mother, and it emerged that Vicky believed her father preferred her friend to her. I wished that I had got help for her at a much earlier time. I wish she had asked questions.'*

Patricia

Dorothy had a similar story. Her daughter was a teenager and became very distressed when her father went away:

*'Eve developed a bad food intolerance from the time of our separation until today. She is now 21 and asthmatic; I believe she has just started therapy to find some answers of her own.'*

Dorothy

# CHILDREN AT DIFFERENT AGES: DIFFERENT EFFECTS AND DIFFERENT QUESTIONS

Problems can arise when there are children of different ages in the family. What may be acceptable to one child may not be so for an older sibling.

*'With the eldest child I said a lot, but in a simplified way. When the others asked questions I said a little, bit by bit.'*

Elizabeth (mother of three children, 6, 4 and 3)

*'I told our eldest right away and we decided together not to tell the little ones until things were more sorted out. Very messy really.'*

Rachel

Opinions were divided about who should tell the children, and whether they should be told individually or together, or indeed by one parent or both (we hear more from the memories of older children of how they heard the news in Chapter 5.)

*'It would never have occurred to Bill to tell the children. He had enough trouble telling me! I decided I had to tell Ben and I took him out in the car and as gently as I could told him, "Daddy wasn't going to live with us any more." He was silent for a bit and then asked if we could go home. I took this to mean that he couldn't take in any more at that moment and he needed to be somewhere familiar and safe. I told Julie, who was just two, on her own too and she was physically sick, and vomited for the rest of the day. She took it really hard, but didn't have the words to express her feelings I suppose.'*

(Marie, mother of Ben, 4, and Julie, 2)

*'Jane walked in on us during one of our rows. She asked, "What's up?", and we told her straight out that we were separating. She howled and rocked herself with the pain. It was terrible – then we had to decide how to tell the boys. Sam couldn't or wouldn't – so I did it next day. It wasn't fair on Jane for her to be the only one who knew.'*

(Sue, mother of Jane, 10 and sons, 8 and 6)

Louise described in Chapter 1 how she felt she had to 'talk, talk talk' at the beginning of the separation; she also said that she felt this must apply to children too. Once she had told them, she tried to give them all some private time with her each day, so that they could ask her questions and, if she could, she would try to answer them. She found it more difficult to find a way of helping her 2½-year-old, Judy. Judy started to walk around carrying a pink pig which had been given to her in happier times by her father. One day Judy told her mother that the pig was unhappy. 'Why?' asked Louise. 'Well,' said Judy, 'people think the pig is big, but it's little inside and needs lots of cuddles.' Louise was pleased that Judy could begin to express some of the feelings she had inside in her own way. Louise could then begin to try to talk 'through' the pink pig to Judy, which Judy enjoyed. Their special time consisted of lots of cuddles and reassurance that everything was all right – Mummy was there and would stay there, to look after Judy and the pig.

Children of all ages needed to be reassured that divorce is a grown-up business and that it is the mother and father who cannot get along, *but* parents keep loving their children. It is only the adults who do not love each other any more.

Louise was able to find a way of communicating with Judy through the pig. Some mothers found it helpful to speak generally and mention other children whose parents were getting divorced sometimes felt unhappy or worried about where Daddy had gone. Even if there is no direct response, it helps children to realise that other children worry about similar issues, and that it is OK to have these worries or feelings.

It is not unusual for a child who has lost the certainty of having both parents at home to begin to fear that the other parent may go too. Even if the father did not see much of the children when he lived at home there was a presence of a father in the house and the children will notice this absence. We were told about children who expressed fears that if they were naughty they would have to leave home, like Daddy.

Parents often hope that children aged 0–3 would not notice and that they might not have to answer the questions that older children might ask. In our experience this is not so.

*'You cannot just do something quickly and hope the children won't notice. My two were 3 years and 20 months old when their father went to live with his new partner. I met someone else too who,*

*because of my fear and loneliness, we subsequently went to live with. I was so stupid, as this was when my problems really began.'*
Sally

*'My marriage was in deep trouble before my second child was born. I was very upset inside, and I don't believe it was chance that my daughter was an unhappy baby and had sleep problems right from the start. I suppose you could say she was the third person to know our marriage was cracking up.'*

Paula

This was backed up by Sandra, whose husband left her two days after her baby was born.

*'I was trying to breastfeed Jason and my husband sat on the bed and said, "I am moving out, I'm leaving you." I said, "I'm sorry?" because I just couldn't believe my ears. He repeated what he had said and I cried and said, "You can't leave us now" – he told me that I was lucky he had stayed until after the birth; he had wanted to leave last summer to live with his secretary.'*

Sandra

In Sandra's words, she 'almost went out of her mind' and the next few weeks passed in a blur. What she does remember, though, is that Jason became a very irritable and colicky baby and she says that can't have been chance. When racking her brains to try to understand what was happening, she found herself turning against Jason. If he hadn't been born . . . In the event her sister looked after Jason for two months to give Sandra time to 'sort herself out'. Six years on, Sandra is very bitter about the way she and Jason missed out on the early months together and the impact this has had upon Jason. Somewhere along the line she made the decision that when Jason is old enough to ask, 'Where is my father?', she will try to ensure that he is not left with the idea that he caused the break-up of the relationship.

What is obvious to adults is not necessarily obvious to a child. Sandra says she continually keeps in mind that Jason needs and will need to be told again and again that they did not get divorced because he was born. Sandra spoke to us of her worries about the effect that Jason's father leaving him at birth might have on Jason in later life. She hoped to be able to help Jason to understand that the divorce had been between two adults and Jason was quite innocent.

*'My daughter Jo was only 20 months when my husband and I parted. He went off to the States, and I told Jo, "Daddy has gone to work in America", but didn't dwell on it. I tried to keep her routine as normal as possible and friends assured me that Jo was far too young to be bothered by the break-up. After all, she could hardly speak, just the odd word. After he had been gone about a month he telephoned to discuss our settlement and after a while I passed the phone to Jo. My husband said "It's Daddy", and Jo became very, very agitated. "Dad, Dad, 'Merica," she cried over and over. Then, to my surprise, "Daddy – see you 'Merica", again and again in a very distressed way. She would not let go of the phone – my husband wept and so did I. We both realised the impact on our little girl. I had no idea she could form a sentence and let her feelings be known so clearly.'*

Anna

*'My son Peter, then aged 14, picked up that things were wrong and he talked about his unhappiness. In his words, "You can have a good day and feel good at school with your friends, and then bang the front door goes and you think Dad is home and we are all going to have an argument." I know the teen years are supposed to be difficult but I do think Peter and his brother, who is two years older, had a very hard time because of the atmosphere at home. It was when considering whether to confront my husband or not I looked at my boys and could see they knew something was wrong and I had to do something about it. When do you know whether you are just going through a bad patch (a very lengthy bad patch) or that you have reached the end of a marriage? They certainly noticed that their father was hardly ever at home. I know that because Peter asked me, "What's wrong with us, Mummy?" I did know there*

*were problems but I'm an optimist and I hoped I'd solve them. After he'd left, Peter said, "Don't even try and get him back – he'd only be grumpy all the time.'*

June

*'I was fretting inside – I knew something was very wrong with our relationship. One day Mark said, "Why are you so sad, Mummy?", and I replied, "Mummy's just being silly." Looking back, what was silly was replying like that. I think I only succeeded in worrying Mark, because I soon noticed that he was very irritable and cried for nothing. My mum told me it was time to have a talk with him and to tell him his dad and I were thinking of living apart.'*

Sally (mother of Mark, 7)

# THE NEED TO KEEP GOING

For many women, their experiences of discovering that their relationship is about to break up include initial shock, disbelief and pain; while they are battling to understand what was happening and what changes were about to take place, they had children to care for.

*'I just kept repeating to myself that I must swim for the sake of the children when in reality I just felt like letting the water close over my head.'*

Bridget

*'I used to wander around the supermarket in a daze; all I knew was I had to get food for the children's tea and it could take me hours to choose something.'*

June

The need to keep life as near normal as possible to help the children feel secure was often paramount, but we wondered whether some women took this to extremes.

*'When Justin told me he had to leave us, I could not tell the children the truth and I told them he had to go to Scotland to work. This was*

*accepted, I think, by them for some time. I thought I was lucky that Justin didn't want to see the children at first, so my lie held water. Looking back, I don't think I was so clever. The children began to pine for Justin and my lies got me into deeper and deeper water. At the time, I thought I was doing the right thing for them, but when I had to tell them the full story, they had to deal with my part in the uncertainty of it all as well as their father going. It was a while before they knew what to believe.'*

Lily

Agnes, however, thought that Lily had it right.

*'I told them Daddy was abroad for a few months. It gave me time to collect myself together. I saw a Relate counsellor and once I felt stronger I could begin to prepare the children over a few weeks for the fact their father had gone. I think it would have been cruel just to blurt it out.*

*'I felt that for the children to have a hysterical mother would terrify them. If I wasn't coping how could I expect my children to be able to? My Relate counsellor helped me to get things in order in my mind and I honestly think I was able to convey to the kids that although Dad had gone, life would go on. It would be different but not necessarily awful.'*

Agnes

(We look further at counselling and other help in Chapter 6.)

# CONCLUSIONS

Some mothers chose not to tell their children about the break-up. Perhaps there was a decision to play for time, in the hope that the husband would come home and the children need never know that he had left. However, we know that children are not oblivious to their surroundings, and to believe that children do not notice when something is wrong is perhaps more about protecting the adult from the knowledge of the child's pain and uncertainty than about the child.

When I was
Little I felt
sick When
Daddy left.

daddy
Leeving
our
house

mummys
home

# Chapter 3

# *Contact and its Problems*

'*The Child is father of the Man.*'

WORDSWORTH

'*Give me the children until they are seven and anyone may have them afterwards.*'

ST FRANCIS XAVIER

Cᴀɴ ᴛʜᴇ path between mothers and fathers be smoothed and made as comfortable as possible for the children? Many parents reported problems with contact. We were soon convinced that for many families the strain around agreement over contact and the actual hand-over from one parent to another was one of the most difficult hurdles of all.

'*On their return from a contact weekend, the children would always be very rude to their father – calling him names and using very unacceptable language. My ex would just smile and say nothing, exactly how he behaved during our marriage, ignoring difficult situations. One day I said to him, "don't let them get away with speaking to you like that", which made me the one to get heavy. I realised just what a tricky time hand-over was. The children were testing the water to see who was in control of a situation in which I knew they felt immune to rules and regulations.*'

Liz

## Fᴇᴇʟɪɴɢs ABOUT CONTACT

'*The first time their father came to the home for contact it was all so difficult. I was still in shock about his leaving us, very distressed.*

42

*The children, very small and perplexed, eventually got into the bath and Matt left. Both children were crying as he went off. Eventually, they were comforted and I got them out of the bath. We went downstairs and there he still was – the children became very upset again as he went out the door. He left behind two hysterical children and a distraught wife.'*

Louise

*'When the children came back from contact days in the beginning it was so hard not to cross examine them: What did you do? Did you like it? What was said? Who was there? If you are close to the children, they answer what you want to hear. Even though my children were so young they could sense what not to say; they didn't want to hurt me.'*

Eileen (mother of two children, 3 and 4)

*'Out of the mouths of babes! One evening after a contact weekend, I went to tuck my daughter (then aged 6) into bed at night and she asked me, "Have you seen my picture?". I looked and saw an unsmiling pin man surrounded by twenty "d's" and hundreds of kisses. I commented that it was nice, but he didn't look very happy. She replied, "He isn't, because of what he's done."'*

Wendy

Louise told us that before she could even think of what was right for the children by way of contact, she had to manage the situation for herself.

*'Sometimes I couldn't cope with him in the house when he came to collect the children and sometimes I would encourage him into the house because I wanted a little piece of what we had had, even though I knew I felt worse afterwards.'*

Louise

Louise went on to tell us how difficult the children found the handover to their father.

*'I found it all so difficult and distressing and the children knew this.
It probably did mean that it was even harder for them to leave me.'*

Louise

As he was always late coming to collect them, the tension and apprehension was considerable before he arrived. Louise also told us that his unreliability, especially over time-keeping, had been a source of great irritation during the marriage. Traits that caused annoyance in the past often enrage after a separation.

*'The children would wait at the window watching out for him and then grow more impatient and irritable as time passed by. I knew just how they felt and could remember only too clearly the hours I had spent waiting for their father to come home. I gradually came to see I had a choice here. Cyril was bound to be late – he always was and if 12 years of marriage hadn't changed him, nothing would. I sat down with the children and told them that Daddy did seem to have a problem with being on time. It was one of the things about Daddy I didn't like. It didn't mean Daddy didn't love them or had forgotten them but they should know he probably always would be late collecting them.'*

Louise

Louise said she thought that it was an important part of helping the children to begin to understand some of the reasons why their parents couldn't live together. Louise felt that as long as she also told the children some of the good things about their father it would enable them to know what to like and what not to like in a person. She laughed as she went on to say she even felt willing to admit to them a few of her own faults and hoped this would make the children have more love and respect for her, not less.

Most women said that they did try to meet 'as a couple' to decide about contact arrangements. The children, though, did not always fit in with the plans agreed.

*'The whole question of access had been very difficult: first my eldest son didn't want to visit him and then my daughter refused. There*

*was always one willing and one not, as if they had an unspoken agreement to make it difficult. I think it was to show us they had feelings.'*

Betty

*'The memory of those early contact days is still a nightmare. As the car drew up, Melinda would shoot upstairs and hide under her bed. At the time my son was quite happy to go with his dad, but Melinda would scream and scream and in the end her father would lose his patience and carry her out of the house. The odd thing was that this went on week after week until one day she went calmly and then, and only then, did her brother rebel about going. I do wonder what they transmitted to each other. My dilemma was should I have said he couldn't take Melinda until she wanted to go – her screams used to be quite dreadful and the memory made me ill for the rest of the day.'*

Paula (mother of a son, 8, and Melinda, 4)

Lucy agreed with Paula that when her child first went off with her dad, she was wiped out for the day. Lucy also got very anxious at the time her daughter was due home. Her fears were that her estranged husband would somehow turn her daughter (3) against her and that Mary might even not want to come back to her. She said that she and her daughter were often a bit awkward with each other upon her return – but the fear when Mary was away from her took many, many months to subside.

*'I was calm enough about their going with their father until I heard of the terrible story of the divorced dad killing himself and his four children. The papers reported that the father gave no signs of mental disturbance, just depression over the divorce and money worries. That was a bit too close to home, and I was unable to settle when they, were away from me for some time. I had to resist the temptation to phone them all the time to check they were OK. I can't bear to think about what that poor woman had to go through.'*

Andrea

We heard, too, that there were problems upon returning home.

*'The first time my two stayed overnight with their father they came home shell-shocked. They had had no preparation to discover their father sleeping in the same bed as his girlfriend: "Just like a mummy and a daddy do," said my youngest daughter. I had all along tried to tell the children simple truths about what was happening. I rang my ex to have a go at him but he said they had better get used to it because his girlfriend was here to stay. When my son heard this he said, "I hate Daddy." I thought this was hard for him to deal with. Probably, he was picking up a lot of my fury so I said, "You don't really hate him, inside you love him." He replied, "Yes, I suppose I do, but on the outside I hate him."'*

Louise (mother of a son, 9, and daughter, 4)

Louise was relieved in a way that Mark could put some of his feelings into words and she said she always kept in mind that they might say things they thought she wanted to hear. That's a heavy burden for any child, and she waited to find a way to help Mark realise that it is possible to have very mixed, often very strong, feelings towards another person. Louise believed passionately that if children's feelings are ignored or are not dealt with they continue to simmer away inside.

In another account, on the way home from sports day, Hilda noticed James was very quiet. They chatted for a while, but James remained unusually monosyllabic. Thinking about the afternoon, Hilda realised that it had been the first school event that James had been to without his father. She thought of asking James if that was why he was quiet, but then something prompted her to wait and see and they drove home in silence. At bath time, James was playing with his boats and suddenly said, 'Oscar's dad ran the fastest.' Hilda felt this was the moment to mention gently that James must have missed his dad today. James was then able to let Hilda know in no uncertain way that he was very angry not to have both parents there. Hilda felt quite shocked to hear how angry he was, and as she listened she realised he felt angry with her for not 'letting' his father come to the sports day. She tried to collect her thoughts – all she could think of was how unfair the attack was and how far from the truth. What Hilda said was, 'I can hear you are very upset about Daddy not being there and that you think it was my fault. I'm sad he wasn't there too. Now, why don't we have an extra story before bed to cheer us both up?' As she tidied up the bathroom, Hilda thought over their conversation and felt pleased that she had given James some room to explore his own thoughts and that holding back in the car it had given her time to think. If she had said in the car, 'I expect you missed Daddy today', James probably would have agreed and the subject – on the surface – would have been closed. By waiting until James was ready to talk, Hilda had understood more about the way he felt about the day, and how he blamed both his parents for his distress. It gave Hilda a great deal to think about: how do you tell a five-year-old boy that his father never asks when sports day or any other event is?

## ROOM FOR FLEXIBILITY?

Contact arrangements can be very difficult for children with full and organised timetables. Is there to be overlap? What about parents' evenings at schools, swimming galas during the week, birthday parties or sports days?

*'I hadn't realised it would not be a once and for all situation. My husband and I worked out a rota for contact and we tried to stick to it. It got more complicated as the children got older and began to be asked out to play or to parties. I believed we should put the children's activities first, but my ex-husband seemed to think it was a plot against him. Yet when he had something on the arrangements could change all right. Only last week he rang and said he had a party to go to on the Friday night, and might be too tired to drive and to get to us by 10 o'clock on the Saturday. The feebleness of that did not go unnoticed by my 11-year-old.'*

Beryl

## UNRELIABLE FATHERS

Many women talked about the problems caused by fathers not being reliable and sticking to the arrangements. Mary told us that

Bob was supposed to have the children some weekends but often simply failed to collect them and did not ring. He did arrive, she calculated, about one or two times in four – just enough to keep them all on tenterhooks. Mary said she would have liked to have cancelled the whole arrangement but she felt it was important for the children to have some kind of contact. To her annoyance, Bob became a kind of Santa Claus; when he did visit, he would come with expensive toys and would make sure the children had a good time when they went out.

*'Access is not frequent. He pops round to see the youngest when he can be bothered and when he wants to question me about my life. The way things are going, it's all going to get worse.'*

Sally

*'Contact did not go as planned for my two children, as their father lost interest when he had a new girlfriend. His visits were to meet his needs, not those of his sons.'*

Belinda

*'My ex was supposed to have the children for the weekend. On the Friday he left a message on my answering machine to say he had to go to Paris on business so had to cancel the plans. My eldest, George, was deeply upset. Later that evening he said: "I bet Dad's gone to see Connie instead of seeing us. Can I ring Connie's number and see if Dad's there?" I felt in my heart that that was where his dad was – with his girl friend. I didn't hesitate and told George he could telephone. His dad, of course, was there – he even answered the 'phone. George was speechless with grief – now he felt he had proof that his dad prefered Connie not only to me but to his children. I still agonise over whether I should have stopped him ringing.'*

Laura

Mary remembered with distress the effect this yo-yo relationship had on the children. She was the one who had to mop up tearful faces, peaky with disappointment, when Bob failed to arrive. On the other hand she had to cope with her own feelings when they went rushing out to him when he did come and when they returned from a 'marvellous, magical trip' and were too excited to go to bed to sleep. One night after such an outing Mary overheard her son talking to his sister about a plan he had to trap his father when he next came to the house – he'd tie him up so he would be unable to leave. Mary sat on the stairs and wept – she said she wondered if it was such a good idea to maintain this kind of pseudo contact, but did she really have a choice? What she did was to have a face-to-face meeting with Bob, which took some organising, and they did agree on contact being reduced to once a month. At the time of writing, Bob is able to manage this. Mary does telephone Bob the day before, to double-check that he will be there, more or less on time.

Mary did have the benefit and support of a counsellor to help her think this through. At first, when Bob didn't turn up, she felt murderous towards him and would storm in front of the children about how uncaring and callous their father always was and still is. It was only when she overheard her son's fantasy and sensed his longing that she decided to consult with a professional and to find a way out of this awful muddle. Mary was able to arrive at a point where she could convince herself – and Bob – that any arrangements they made must be for the good of the children. Bob realised that he could not go on pretending, even to himself, that he really would keep up very regular and frequent contact. Once Mary had understood the pressure she had been under in trying to deal with her own unresolved feelings about Bob and the way he had left her, she was then more able to look at the effect split and access arrangements were having on the children. Only then could she stand to one side and see that the children were being torn apart by their parents inability to work out an access agreement which Bob could keep to. Mary felt free to make plans for the weekends when Bob was not visiting and began to appreciate and accept the help of the extended family. It was a much calmer way of dealing with the situation and the children marked the visiting dates on the calendar – meanwhile they were free as a family to enjoy themselves. It was different to be sure, but good, they all agreed.

*'Jack so wanted his dad at his birthday party – the first one after we separated. After a lot of thought I let Jack invite him but I told Jack that Daddy would probably be "too busy" to come. I knew his dad too well you see. Of course he didn't turn up and I could see that Jack had his eye on the door most of the time; the unspoken question on his face was "Where's Daddy?".'*

Barbara

When Barbara was asked why she had let Jack invite his father when she knew he would be let down, she explained:

*'Jack has to learn from experience, his own experience. I knew it, but if I'd vetoed the invitation Jack would have believed I was the one stopping his father from coming.'*

Barbara

*'My ex husband has never had much regard for time; he was always late everywhere and for everyone. He was late, very late, for our first date, and with hindsight perhaps I shouldn't have been still standing there 45 minutes after the arranged time. But I was, and ten years later, the result is an ex husband and our children being returned later than arranged after every contact day. I try hard to stay calm, but when Bill and Tina come home late again and again, overtired on a Sunday evening, and I have to say, "There are spellings to learn and it's too late for a video before bed", I feel very much the bad guy. I've tried talking to Fred, but all he says is, "tea was late, the riding lesson went over time, there was bad traffic on the roads," or, "it's because of the rain". I ask myself where's the good parenting in this? Nine times out of ten, the children phone me from the car en route, crying or fussing, saying they want me: that's because it's late. It's been a stressful/exciting day and they are tired children, often hungry and bored in the back of the car in the dark. Through my mind goes a subterfuge that I the three of us will not to be here when he comes to pick them up? How will that help the children, let alone the*

*situation? I spent 10 years hanging around for this man and despite the divorce, I am still hanging around for him. If I was late back because "they are always late", it would probably be the first time they were back early and the children would be worried that I wasn't here for them. This would be much harder for them to understand because it would be so out of character for me. Is it better then to be predictable, despite the cost?'*

Fiona

Fiona and Fred may be at a stage where punishment of the other parent is still the name of the game. All unresolved feelings seemed to be focused on the point of contact and this must be very difficult for the children, who would probably feel responsible for the tensions that arise between the parents at the moment when the children are passed from one to the other. We hoped that Fiona and Fred would continue to discuss the problem quietly and privately together in the hope that a truce can be called and parenting (and acknowledgement of the pressures in the children's world) can be the prime object. Fiona and Fred have yet to come to terms with the power struggle over the children and contact time. Fiona disagreed with our comments and maintained that if Fred kept to time, all would be well.

Sue said her arguments with her children's father were about the time they agreed he would bring them home.

*'It was always later and the children arrived home fractious and overwrought, and often hungry. When tackled on this Burt would say vaguely, "Oh, they've had crisps and things." That just about summed up his view of being a parent.'*

Sue

Sue wondered if Burt's attitude was a way of getting back at her? Why else would he subject the children to a longer than planned weekend which left everyone upset? Any attempt to discuss the situation with Burt was met by an onslaught of bullying – very reminiscent of her married life, she thought.

*'Contact was not good after he left. I had to remind my ex-partner of his responsibilities as a father and insist on his keeping in touch with the children.'*

Penny

Penny's husband showed no interest in seeing the children after he left their home but Penny kept in mind the harm this could do her daughters and continually insisted he make, and keep, arrangements for them to visit. He was their father and needed to be reminded of this.

A considerable number of people replied to the question, 'How was access/contact decided?' with a brief, 'by the courts'.

*'Tom's dad fought for custody but he was granted access which he used two or three times, but was very unreliable about bringing Tom home. I had to stop access at this point to relieve the pressure on the whole family. He has never contested this.'*

Connie

*'My husband was totally unreliable and lied throughout our marriage. I am like a ton of bricks onto my kids at the first sign of them not keeping a promise or being late. They think I am very strict, but I know I have to draw the line.'*

Vikki

## PRESSURE ON THE WHOLE FAMILY

Not only the immediate family has difficulties with contact days. We heard from one grandmother who told us about her feelings when her grandsons were collected by their father.

*'My ex son-in-law hooted outside and my daughter buttoned up the boys' coats, hugged them and opened the door for them to go out to their father. We shut the door as they wandered off to their father's car, but something made me go back to the door and I saw through the glass that Luke had come back and was standing at the shut door unsure whether to go forward or back. I opened the door and*

*he said, "Oh, Grandma, I just wanted to give you a kiss goodbye."
After he had gone I felt sick and had more of an idea what my
daughter was going through every contact day.'*

(Grandmother of two boys, 9 and 11)

The knowledge of a contact day or weekend approaching would
begin to cast a shadow over the lives of some families for days
beforehand.

*'I found it affected the way I handled the children – I'd begin to get
tense at the thought of them going away, but at the same time would
begin to go easy on the kids because I didn't want them to go to their
father and say I was a witch. In reality what happened was that I
would be different and the kids would pick this up, their behaviour
would alter and I'd end up shouting. The very thing I'd set out to
avoid.'*

Tracy

*'My ex was very strict about table manners whilst I have a pretty
relaxed attitude. However, when they came back week after week
telling me they had been punished for what I consider petty things I
did wonder if I should tighten up on them to make things easier for
them on contact days. We had never seen eye to eye on discipline or
on any aspects of child care, so I'm not suprised we differ now. All
week I worry about the next Sunday.'*

Pat

*'I found that the more the children protested in advance about a
contact visit, and kept asking questions about when the day was
coming, and made comments such as, "I don't want to see Daddy, I
hate Daddy's cooking", and, "We never get to do what we want", the
more prepared they were when their father came for them. They even
asked on many occasions, "Why can't you come too?". I often wished
that my ex could hear and see this preparation, together with the
intense kissing and hugging that went on before his arrival. I felt torn
inside. As a mother, of course I wanted to deal with the handover as
easily as possible for them but at the time inside I was still very bitter*

*about the way my ex had destroyed my family life. It used to make my blood boil that he appeared to think it was all too easy. And he even wanted more. It's all very well to try to deal with these occasions in a calm and collected way. On one level I believe that, but please remember emotions run very deep and it's not always possible to rise above them and to say and do the right thing at the right time.'*

Gloria

*'There were so many differences between us, money, access new partners. Something had to change. One evening after I had put the phone down on my ex, knowing he and his new partner were at home, I turned up on their doorstep and said, "lets talk". Although I will never like Jo-Ann, she does, after all, look after my little girl on alternate weekends. I suppose it's best that I accept her. Because my ex now sees I held out the white flag for the future he is less aggressive at contact times and has even stopped threatening me about money. It took me a long time to get over the meeting, but on balance I think it was the only, and the right, thing to do.'*

Gwen

# OTHER DIFFICULTIES FOR THE RESIDENT PARENT

The parent with the custody of the children has other problems as well.

*'After we divorced, we moved South to be nearer my family. Six months later, our new next door neighbours told me they had been very anxious when they learnt that a single parent with children was moving in. They had expected the worst, they said, and very unruly children.'*

Carol

*'I got to know another mother from my daughter's school and, after a while, told her I was divorced. She looked shocked and blurted out "But your girls are so well behaved and happy". Single parents get a bad press, I'm afraid.'*

Peg

'I had the children during the week and both my daughters hated it if I had anyone to visit in the evening. They watched me closely. They never knew, of course, who their dad saw during the week. It made me feel I had to justify my actions.'

Millie

'Once I had begun to surface again, I started to date. In fact I had three or four men I was seeing socially. I made a bit of a joke to my son, saying that I had more boyfriends now than when I was a young girl. My son looked at me hard and said, "Perhaps you should tell a couple of them you can't go out because you need to spend more time with your children." That from a nine year old.'

Susie

'I had many dates, but nobody special for a couple of years. When I did meet a man I felt I might get involved with, I told the children I had met a "special friend", to give the children a hint that he might be around in our lives in time and that there was something different in the air.'

Kathleen

'When my children went off with their dad for the weekend he would ask for my telephone number so I could be reached. I began to see this as a great restriction and control over my life – so I asked him to lend me his mobile phone so I could be contacted without his knowing my every movement. A taste of his own medicine and freedom for me.'

Millie

Many women felt they were under the scrutiny of their former partner and this often added to the tension at home on either side of contact. We were shown that the difficulty for some women focused on how they looked. Many felt caught in a Catch-22 situation: if they looked depressed or unkempt they felt they were often despised or perhaps contrasted with the newer, and often younger, partner. On the other hand, if they looked confident and happy ex-partners become jealous or aggressive.

Another problem is that as well as feelings running very high at hand-over time, it often becomes a forum for discussion over money or other unresolved issues.

Pat wanted us to pass on this plea to anyone on the brink of making arrangements for the children:

*'If I could pass on one thing to someone in this position it would be: bite your tongue, stitch up your lips but don't argue in front of the children.'*

Pat

# STRESS ON THE CHILD
Children are often under stress around contact time, both before and afterwards.

*'When Gary and Mark came home from an "overnight" with their father they looked tired and strained. I estimated that they had been driven over 200 miles: first to their father's new home and then to his parents. I reminded them that they had homework for school the next day and Gary burst into tears. Now, Gary is not a cry baby and I took his distress seriously. He said he felt he hadn't had a weekend and it couldn't be Monday tomorrow. My heart went out to a small boy trying to bridge two worlds.'*

Joyce (mother of two sons, 11 and 13)

*'When Joe went to his father's house, he wouldn't eat – he said he didn't like the food. I know my husband tried to cook like he thought I did, but it was no good, Joe would not eat. My ex-husband would telephone me to question me about what foods Joe ate at home. I couldn't understand the problem as Joe wasn't a fussy child. Months later, it emerged that meal times with Joe's father and his new partner were a great source of stress, both being very hot on good behaviour at the table.'*

Jane

*'After three years of our wrangling about access, our son had just begun to look forward to seeing his father at weekends. Then one*

*day Richard, who was 5 at the time, came back home looking shocked and pale. My ex said he'd given him a clip round the ear because Richard had been rude to the new woman in his life. Later that evening my son told me his dad had told him his new partner was having a baby. My ex, of course, made no connection between the news of the pregnancy and my son being upset.'*

Wendy

*'I got so angry with Annie. During the week she would cry at bedtime and say she was missing her dad. When he came for her on a Sunday, she would create a huge fuss about going with him and on her return would tell me she'd had a horrid time. After a day or two it would all start up again, and always at bedtime.'*

Rowena (mother of Annie, 6)

Annie had been very small when Bill left the family and it is possible that she missed, and was crying for, a fantasy father rather than her own dad. When she was with him, she was disappointed. Rowena said that although she had not looked at it in this way she felt it might be true. Understanding more about the reasons behind her daughter's behaviour helped Rowena to be less impatient and bewildered by Annie's seemingly erratic behaviour and confused feelings.

*'My 8-year-old son suddenly became very clumsy, falling out of a tree, crashing his bike and banging his head. It occured to me that it may all be deliberate when one day he had scratches on his face. A few nights after this last incident he started to cry as I put him to bed. After some talking I asked Freddie if he was missing his daddy? He said "no" and started to cry again, saying he never wanted to see him ever again. Freddie told me that was why he was hurting himself, "So that Daddy would say he didn't want to see such an ugly boy." I was so shocked I was speechless, then I pulled myself together and told him that his father would always love him whatever he looked like. I knew he wanted reassurance that his daddy did still love him even though he had left the home.'*

Tricia

Freddie's experience shows just how hard a child finds it to deal with family separations, and the dilemma of trying to understand why his parents do not love each other any more. If that can happen, will they stop loving him?

Some children have very strong clear feelings about the amount of contact with their father – whereas others are ambivalent and express these mixed feelings in different ways.

*'I miss Daddy now, but when I am with him I miss Mummy; what I really want is to see Mummy and Daddy together.'*

Tim (7)

*'Hearing him say that broke my heart.'*

Carol (mother of Tim)

Polly remembered her daughter of 2½ screaming each time her father arrived to take her out for the day. Polly tried in different ways to make it easier for Helen, but each time it was the same. When Helen was five and, at times, still became very distressed, Polly decided enough was enough. Helen was old enough to know if she really did not want to go with her father that day. Polly talked to Helen, in front of Helen's dad, and pointed out to her that if she did not go she wouldn't see her dad for a week.

*'That's all right. I do miss you, Daddy, but I don't want to spend the day with you.'*

Helen

Polly felt that if she had not let her ex-husband take Helen off – crying – when she was small, in years to come Helen might well have believed that she had had no contact with her father because Polly had prevented it. Or, indeed, that Bill had not wanted it. By the time Helen was five, she herself had a clearer idea of when she did or did not wish to see her father, and could have some say in, and responsibility for, what she wanted. Polly felt it could only be very harmful psychologically if everyone continued to ignore what Helen was saying. However, as time went on, Polly kept on explaining to Helen just what was happening and each time Bill arrived to collect Helen they decided together whether it was one of those days when Helen should be encouraged to spend time with her father or, if she was really upset, to stay at home. This was practical because Bill lived only two streets away. Polly feels that in the future Helen will know that her feelings were listened to and taken seriously, and that she did have some choice in whether or not to build a relationship with her father and his new family. If contact had ended when she was only 2½, Helen may well have looked back and seen a very different view. If Bill had truly become an absent father this might have left a psychological hole inside Helen which then may have become filled with resentment, guilt, mistrust and idealisations. An absent father can be both physically and psychologically absent.

# THE NEED FOR A FATHER

How important is it to have two parents involved with a child?

In 1950 the celebrated paediatrician and psychoanalyst, D.W. Winnicott, wrote about the importance of the father in the earliest years of childhood. Until then, recognition of the standing of the mother/child relationship had meant some neglect of the value of the father. Dr Winnicott stressed the significance of the role of the father to protect and support the mother, freeing her to devote herself to the baby. Without this support, the mother has to be involved with the day-to-day worries plus the care of her baby. If a mother of a young child is caught up in the stress of a faulty partnership this does have a profound effect on the quality of the mother/child relationship and also influences the child's perception of the parents. A mother preoccupied with survival or in a disintegrating relationship will have less mental space for the child. In short, less time for the child. If, in addition, the mother denigrates the task of the father this can confuse the child about the necessity of men in one's life.

*'I was happy for them when they went off with their dad for a day – they needed to see him. Although I found the house horribly silent and empty after they'd gone. I was always very glad to see them back. It*

*was dreadful though, Clara would cry when leaving me in the
morning and then cry again in the evening when leaving her dad.'*

Antonia

Even today, some fathers take little or no part in the daily
routines of their children – either because of work commitments
or by choice. Yet their children do not necessarily see this as lack
of love for them and they can still feel loved and secure.

*'I see my dad more often on visits than my friend John sees of his dad
who lives at home but works away a lot. When John's dad is at home
he wants to be with John's mum.'*

Timmy (8) whose parents are divorced

*'At least when Dad spends time with me it is because he wants to
and is interested in me. Amelia's dad lives with her, but he never
takes her out or spends time with her.'*

Joy (12) with separated parents

*'My dad looked after me a lot when I was a baby – it was my mum
who went out to work. Now he's gone and I really miss the things we
did together.'*

Pamela (14)

*'I do love you, Daddy, and I am pleased that I have a daddy. It's just
I don't always want to spend time with you at the weekends, is that
clear?'*

Sara (5)

During the therapy of both children and adults what frequently
emerges is a description of an inner emptiness – a kind of gap to
be filled.

Carrie, 29, a successful solicitor decided to find a therapist to
help her to understand why, although she was happy in her
professional life, her private life was bleak and empty. Her father
had left home when Carrie was 5 years old, and contact with him
had been infrequent over the years. Carrie's mother was very

bitter about the way her husband had left them and never lost an opportunity to belittle or to undermine her former husband. In other words, 22 years on, Carrie's mother continued to hold on to the role of victim and never let a moment pass without bemoaning the fact that men were untrustworthy.

Carrie talked about her own very busy lifestyle, with every hour of the day taken up. In her therapy Carrie began to understand that even her choice of career had been decided (unconsciously) in order to give herself a firm and solid platform to stand on. Carrie had earned the respect of a male-dominated practice and she could hold her own, professionally. Understanding that her total preoccupation with the next event or activity was a way of avoiding her feelings, helped her to create a mental space for her to identify the 'gap' she felt inside. Over the years, she realised, she had at times searched, through sexual encounters, for a relationship with an idealised father who would banish – once and for all – the sense of emptiness. When she had been unsuccessful, she had turned all her attention to achieving recognition at work. Certainly, the approval of the senior partner at work was extremely important to her. However, in the small hours there was no peace of mind for her.

Her relationship with her mother had been fraught with problems and Carrie, as a child, had had difficulty in expressing her anger directly towards her mother. Effectively, having only one parent led her to want to protect her mother from her rage. With only one parent she had 'all her eggs in one basket'. To quote Winnicott: 'Besides, it is much easier for children to be able to have two parents: one parent can be felt to remain loving whilst the other is being hated, and this in itself has a stabilising influence.' Carrie took a long, hard look at her experience with men. On the one hand – at work – she could value their knowledge and reliability. However, on the other, in a more intimate setting she doubted their dependability while continuing to long for, and to search for, an idealised relationship with a man. She recalled thinking as a child that if her father had been so awful (according to her mother) why did her mother constantly moan about the fact her husband had left them? (We look further at psychotherapy in Chapter 6.)

If parents can agree that a father – even part-time – is of importance and value for a child's well-being, this can help both of them to find ways of keeping a place for the father in the child's life.

## SHARED CARE

We heard of a father who left because he wanted space and a new life: this meant it was not on the cards to negotiate time to spend with the children.

There are many fathers who leave because they do not want to live with the mother any more, but love their children dearly and want to see them as much as possible (Chapter 12 discusses this in more detail). They wish they could live with their children and are very sorry to leave them. Some couples can work out a real shared-care situation – where parenting really is joint and there are no divisions between a 'play' and 'work' parent. Unhappily, we did not find this situation very often and we were told again and again of the resentment by the mother who assumes responsibility for taking the children to the dentist whereas the father takes them to the zoo.

Lional, however, told us with very strong feelings:

*'It is no joke trying to think up things to do with your kids. I would have loved to be involved with them during the week – taking them to the dentist and having their hair cut. It just didn't work out that way.'*

Lional

*'When my wife left me she took the girls, but because of her late hours of work, I had them back the next day to look after. Now we live in two houses very close together and have shared care. It works out to be about 50/50 and we plan one month ahead at a time. We feel very strongly that consistency is the main aim here and school and the childminder stay the same. I don't talk to the girls about the situation, I don't want to upset them. They seem fine but then you don't really know about inside, do you?'*

Alan

We asked Alan if his ex wife was happy with shared-care, and he said that she hated it but could not do anything about it because of her work.

One questionnaire was completed by both parents and described how they had cooperated together for the sake of their child.

> 'We married very young and we grew up at different rates. We wanted different things, but we shared a son.'
>
> (Cooperating couple, parents of Joe, 9)

They reorganised their living accommodation into two separate flats and had worked out a real shared-care arrangement. Joe appeared to deal with this reorganisation and had indeed been involved and consulted all along the way. This couple did add that they were mindful of the fact that if one of them became involved with someone else, the balance they had worked out might just not hold.

## SUCCESSFUL CONTACT

> 'Right from the start we all knew where we stood. The children lived with me – but rain or shine they spent every other weekend with their dad.'
>
> Ruby

> 'I was always pleased when the girls went to their father for the day. It gave me a break and I could think of myself.'
>
> Maggie

Jean had very strong views on contact between her daughter and her father.

> 'I worked very hard at making sure contact took place very regularly and that Susie talked on the phone to her father. I never criticised him to her, although some painful facts could not be concealed or denied. Contact was negotiated between us and a solicitor – I insisted he had to see her. Susie was consulted over

*contact in the sense that I gave her permission to see him: it was not disloyal to me if she wanted to, and did, see him; it was OK. I know Susie found it difficult to make the transition between the two of us. On her return, I had to be particularly careful. She needed time on her return to adjust to being at home and liked to be left alone, even after an eight-hour visit. I always tried to answer all my Susie's questions honestly.'*

(Jean, mother of Susie, 8)

Jean felt that contact was particularly hard on Susie as an only child. She could see that a friend of hers in a similar situation felt comforted that when contact time came around for her two boys, they did have each other. Jean's friend June believed that however difficult it was for the children to go from one home to the other they could grumble to each other about their parents and she knew they did. Susie, on the other hand, had to digest her feelings on her own. Jean was sensitive to her daughter's need for some private time and when she noticed Susie seemed particularly stressed and was biting her nails, she did arrange for her to see a child psychotherapist.

*'I know we are close, but I do think that Susie must have things to say which she may hesitate to say to me. If she had a grandmother or favourite aunt, perhaps they could have stepped in – I was very conscious of Susie being a very 'only' and 'solitary' child. Handling contact has been hard work but I still say its been successfull.'*

Jean

*'The children were old enough to arrange to see their father as often as they liked. It worked OK.'*

Janice

These are some examples of less stressful contact. Could it be that the parents in these families were able to stand firm about arrangements made for the children despite their own feelings?

*'All the arrangements were made with the children in mind. We*

*both agreed on that. After all, access is for the children not for the parents.'*

Margaret

Indeed, perhaps leading from the front, with the children picking up on their parents' example, did ease the tension. Finally:

*'What problems with contact? They still had a mum and dad and had to have time with us both.'*

Ruby

Dear Daddy
when can I see you

# Chapter 4

# *Reconciliation and its Aftermath*

---

*'But I do love thee — and when I love thee not, chaos is come again.'*

SHAKESPEARE

*'The worst reconciliation is preferable to the best divorce.'*

CERVANTES

O<small>NE VERY</small> difficult situation for children is where the parent who leaves does come back home to stay, only to leave again.

*'A week after Paul went, I woke in the middle of the night with a raging temperature. I had 'flu really badly. I was alone with three small children so I rang Paul and told him he had to come home. He did, but it didn't work out, and I know he was very resentful and angry with me. As soon as I was better he was off again and has always thrown it back to me that I couldn't cope. I think it was puzzling for the children too. Looking back I think it was really the shock of it all that made me ill. After he left the second time I became very depressed.'*

Diana

*'My partner returned three times. The length of time varied between four and seven days. The children seemed pleased to see him back, but obviously after the third time they were confused and disturbed when he decided he would leave once again. I realised that I could*

*not go through this ever again for my children's sake and for myself.'*

Paula

'*Ted returning and leaving again did confuse the children as it built up hopes that were then dashed again. My youngest was particularly affected: "Why can't I have both of you?" she'd cry again and again.'*

Sandy

'*My husband left, but came back to see the children in the home on Wednesday nights and alternate weekends: this went on for 2½ years. For me this was a very difficult time; we were separated in one sense but still physically together. The children saw us with a bad relationship but couldn't grieve the ending of it because in a sense he was still there. My youngest son was only able to recognise the ending of the relationship when his father finally moved out.'*

Irene

'*A week after Eric walked out he rang and asked to come back. I said OK, and was prepared to forget everything and work things out. Two months later it all started again. This time he sneaked in while I was taking the children to school and packed most of his things and left. We were all bewildered and very hurt. I didn't know what to tell the children.'*

Mavis

'*After a silence of two years, Billy rang and asked to meet me in the park. I went with my youngest and Billy said he loved me and wanted to come home. I was on cloud nine. Then he told me he'd just received the divorce papers from my solicitors, and he didn't want our marriage to end. He said he'd sort things out with the kids. It didn't last, and the kids were ever so upset.'*

Patti

'*We tried a reconciliation three times. The last time he left me I packed up all his things and took them to where he worked. I couldn't take it any longer and neither could my daughter.'*

Liz

*'The youngest was pleased that he came back, but when her father left again – that's when the real trouble started.'*

Matilda

*'After he left the second time my daughter said she would never forgive him, and she hasn't.'*

Hope

*'When Paul wanted to come back the kids said "no" but I thought they'd get used to it. My eldest kept his distance and hardly spoke to either of us. The reconciliation lasted two weeks.'*

Tracy

*'I had very little self-esteem after Jock left me, returned, and then left again. I tried to keep everything the same at home – it was very exhausting when Phil and Maureen became too stroppy and hard to handle. They became super-critical of me, especially after he left the second time; it was the very last thing I needed. Luckily, I had a friend who is a social worker and she lent me a book which went some way to explaining that it was the children's way of letting me know how insecure they were feeling. So OK, my head understood, but I still found it an uphill task to deal with their nagging and whining when I felt so low. I felt useless as a wife, and now as a mother.'*

Christine (mother of Phil, 8, and Maureen, 10)

Christine went on to say that it took a lot of talking with her friend for her to understand that if she could think separately about their behaviour, and about the reason why they were so unsettled, she would deal with their crying and fighting more easily. In other words, she should decide what was acceptable behaviour and what was not, and act on that, rather than wondering if she 'should' or 'should not' make a stand because she is now on her own with them and they were all upside down. The children needed to feel Christine was strong, and they both badly needed her to be firm but clear about what she expected from her children. Christine pointed out how difficult this was at a time when she could hardly get herself up and dressed in the mornings. As life gradually became calmer and Christine was able to take stock, she became more capable of talking to and listening to the children again. She knew they were unhappy because their father was not at home and she did acknowledge that when they could find the words to express all kinds of feelings (some good and some bad) the atmosphere at home felt better and in turn Christine and the children were happier.

> 'Before we got to that point there were lots of tears and raised voices. I was lucky: my friend Pearl would come round whenever I rang her and told her I was desperate. At times, I think she must have thought I was part of her case load, but she was a good friend at a time I really needed one.'

Christine

## MENDED MARRIAGES?

Can a marriage continue after a separation – perhaps after even more than one parting?

> 'Yes, it can if you both are sure that despite all that has happened your future is together. Really it has got to be about you both and not only for the sake of the children.'

Janet

> 'Bob and I had a terrible two years – he left us and returned, three times. The last time he did this we decided to have another child to show our commitment to each other. This time it has lasted but, only last week, our youngest asked if she had been a "patch-up kid" as someone had told her she had been born to try to save our marriage. I suspect it was my eldest boy who said it. I know he suffered badly from those troubled years.'

Laura

Lucy discovered that her husband was having an affair only after the woman he was seeing telephoned her to ask her to 'let David go' as the deception was destroying him. Lucy made a decision not to give David up. She was convinced he had got out of his depth in this relationship and didn't want to leave their marriage and the children, or he would have said something. Lucy told David she knew about the woman and that he was to 'go off working' for a month to get her out of his system; then he would come back to the family and all would be forgotten and forgiven.

This is what happened and life goes on. The few friends of Lucy's who knew what was going on were sceptical asking, 'How will you ever trust him again?', 'Will the other woman just go away?' and 'How can you be sure of anything any more?'. Lucy and David go together weekly to a Relate counsellor and are slowly learning to live and love together again. When Lucy looks at her four children she knows she has done the right thing. But she can't help remembering that terrible time when the children kept asking whether their daddy was coming home. Why be proud? She has got the husband she wants and the life she had planned for.

> *'It is possible but it's not the same and never can be however much we all pretend; still, it's better than the alternative.'*
>
> Debbie

> *'Maybe deep down I knew our marriage wasn't sound but staying all together suits us both and so why not?'*
>
> Joan

> *'Peter and I both had affairs before and after the children were born and I suppose really we are past that need of thrills now and so are just getting down to a busy family life together.'*
>
> Naomi

These families perhaps show that as long as both partners are willing to make a marriage work anything is possible. These are examples of couples who feel they were right to ignore or work through problems; with hindsight many people wish that they had stayed with their original partners, if they had had the chance.

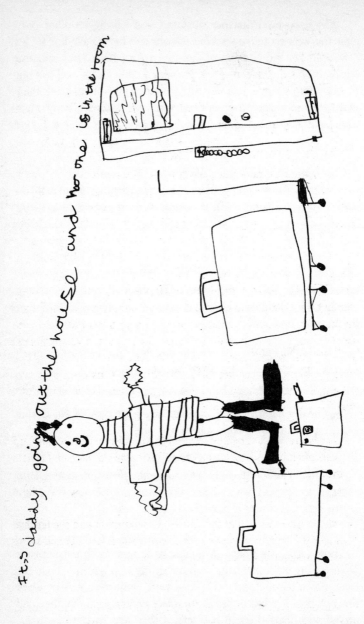

It's daddy going out the house and her one is in the room

# Chapter 5
# *Children of Divorce Speak up*

---

*'A civilized divorce is a contradiction in terms.'*
*The War of the Roses* (film)

*'And the King said, Divide the living child in two,*
*and give half to the one, and half to the other.'*
1 Kings 3:25

## LISTENING TO ADOLESCENTS
Adolescents can find the break-up of their family particularly hard to manage, but many shrug off any offers to talk or of help with their feelings. It may be they will greet the news in a very dramatic way: 'I'll kill myself!', or, 'I really really hate you both!', or, as one parent reported to us, 'Jeremey (16) looked at us both and said, "Right, thanks a lot, you know that means I'll be screwed up don't you?"'

*'They were affected mainly in the split loyalty sphere. They still [15 years on] find it difficult to talk to me about the situation and tend to avoid the subject.'*

Beth

*'My daughter was 16 at the time of the separation and she has had major difficulty in accepting the divorce. She is now 32 and seems loath to commit herself in relationships.'*

Sue

Susannah was 14 when her parents told her they had decided not to live together any more. She remembers that although one part of her seemed to understand what they were saying, another part of her went into free fall. She remembers being very embarrassed by any mention of her parents' decision.

*'I didn't have to ask, "Where's Daddy?" I had it all explained to me, and I knew where he would live and when I would see him. I sat and listened, I didn't cry, but I felt drenched by a feeling of betrayal. I looked down at my shoes when Mum would talk to friends, or neighbours who would ask after Dad – it was so awful, I thought everyone was talking about us.'*

Susannah

*'I was 16 when my parents split up. Dad had an affair and Mum found out. It was an awful time – my Mum was very depressed and Dad didn't seem too happy either. They said I was old enough to work out for myself who I stayed with and how often I saw the other parent. I was so miserable, it felt as if I had a clenched fist in my chest and I couldn't eat. I liked your questionnaire. I think at the time I was affected in all the ways you listed, and I still have dreadful eating problems.'*

Hilary

Adolescence is a particularly difficult time in the growing-up process – and for teenagers to bear, in addition to this, the trauma of parents at war can be a tremendous burden.

One adolescent felt strongly that she was suffering from being divided between her parents:

*'I hate having separated parents. It means they both feel that at weekends they have to do things with me – I'd much rather wander round the shops with my friends or just hang about. But no, because they both work during the week, Mum wants to be with me all Saturday and Dad wants me Sunday. I think they have both read about quality time and it makes them feel good if they have clocked up time with me. I wish they would just be parents and leave me alone.'*

Bessie (16)

*'I was 17 when my dad left home. I went round to see him and said I thought he ought to stay with Mum and he said to me, "Watch it – I've already cut her out of my life – I can cut you out too." I haven't seen him since, and that was five years ago. I don't see much of Mum either, though I do see my Gran. I certainly don't want an answer to "Where's Daddy?".'*

Brian

This response to the question, 'Where's Daddy?', was echoed by a number of the adult 'children' we spoke to.

## ADULTS REMEMBERING

Perhaps before we look any further at the different ways of answering the questions around, 'Where's Daddy?', we should hear the view of some of the adult 'children' we spoke to and try to learn from them.

*'I grew up knowing my parents were unhappy together. They tried to hide it, but my mother's red eyes often told a different story. I used to lie awake in bed and put my head under the pillow when I heard raised voices. I never went to sleep until all was quiet in their room. To this day I have trouble sleeping and cannot get to sleep unless there is absolute silence. I feel safe then, I guess.'*

Jim

*'We knew Dad had a girlfriend – my mates used to see him out with her. They used to tease me a lot. I pretended not to care and I never asked questions.'*

Alec

*'I knew there was trouble long before I was told. I could never risk bringing people home because of the arguing.'*

Joanna

*'I did not think the divorce did affect me but as I get older I realise more and more that it has. I sought friends who did not have fathers*

*because I didn't know what to expect or what they were there for. I felt uncomfortable when there was a dad around.'*

Becky (18, was 18 months when her parents separated)

As she was talking she said the phrase 'mum and dad' and went on to say she hadn't said these words together very often and they didn't sound at all right like that.

*'My mother got divorced three times. I was the child of the first marriage. I didn't think it was the initial divorce which hurt me but the subsequent ones.'*

Monica (19)

When Brian left home, he left a distraught and very depressed wife, and two teenage daughters who were caught in the cross-fire. Loyalty was divided. We heard from Jane and Judy.

*'My sister and I made a pact – if one stayed with Mum, the other went out with Dad. They kept saying to us, "You still have two parents who love you", but it didn't feel like that to us.'*

Jane (then 14, now 24)

*'Jane and I tried to keep the balance and the peace. We got really sick of it – passing messages back and forth – Dad became "your father" and we really felt we were disloyal if we came back from Dad and we had enjoyed ourselves. When I was 20 (and Jane 18) we decided enough was enough. We said we wouldn't be part of it any longer. We called a meeting and told our parents that if they couldn't be our parents we would have nothing to do with them. We let them get on with it and hardly see them now.'*

Judy (then 16, now 26)

It appears that some parents cannot separate their relationships as quarrelling partners from their role as parents. In this situation, it was the children who almost had to parent their parents and say, 'Stop it – we cannot continue like this.' Judy told us that she is sad not only because she and her sister lost their family life when they were teenagers, but her own children are being deprived of grandparents.

*'Being the daughter of a lone parent has certainly affected my life. My Dad left us when I was 3 and I only have a very hazy memory of him. I'm not sure if I asked questions then, but I know I did later. Mum was always very reticent about talking about him. Questions would often be met by silence, which made me feel I'd done something awful. Once, I asked Mum, "Didn't he love either of us?", and she replied, "What do you think?". I know teenagers love to live out a drama, but I did feel a gap in my life without a dad. I know I used to daydream a lot about who he might be. The worst times were when Mum and I fell out, and I'd feel really, really scared on my own. We were very close, my mum and me – and I hated to leave her to go away to stay with friends, and then I would get angry with her because I felt so wretched. Of course, I didn't connect these feelings at the time with feelings about my dad. I had a lot of problems getting to know boys and was very, very shy. There were major events in my life when I'd miss him more – like my graduation and my wedding. I felt dreadful then leaving my mum to start my new life. My husband was very understanding, but it was, at times, as if it was Mum and me who were the couple. I used to feel sad about not having a father; now I just feel angry he left us in the way he did.'*

Erica (now married with a child)

Erica expressed her feelings about the pressure of living with one parent during her early years very clearly. In psychoanalytic terms, without a father she had not had the opportunity to work through her strong loving feelings about a man in the context of an intact parental relationship. It is likely that Erica's situation encouraged the fantasy – common to all children – about wanting a special closeness with her father. However, as her mother continued to express very mixed feelings about her ex-husband, Erica may have been confused and was certainly denied the opportunity of a resolution of her feelings, by accepting the reality of her parents as the couple. Acceptance of this fact helps to free a child to move on and find his or her own partner.

*'I remember just after Dad left I didn't want to go to school. I had tummy ache and my mother tried to persuade me, but I said I was too ill. My mum had to go to work and she tried to find someone to look after me and couldn't. She put down the telephone and started to cry – I was suddenly terrified, and said, "I'll go, I'll go", and I did.'*

Celia (26)

Celia went on to talk about that time, which she can remember vividly, and agreed she must have been very frightened of rocking the boat even more than her father had done when he left. She said she found it hard to be angry with her mum. The only one in the family who had got cross had been her dad and where had that got them all? Into a lot of hot water. In adult life Celia often suffered from depression, and she told us of her surprise when a psychiatric social worker she was seeing asked her if she saw any connection with keeping a tight reign on her feelings and emotions, and her bouts of depression. Celia acknowledged that she did bottle up her feelings. She felt angry or disagreeable feelings were totally unacceptable, and had set out in her teens – quite consciously – to be good, and to oil the wheels in her family. Somewhere along the way she had lost touch with how she was feeling, and her own emotions merged into a bleak, grey depression.

*'My father left when I was 7. My mother wouldn't accept it – and never discussed the situation. She had to go out to work and years later when she retired I couldn't understand why she had such a small pension. All those years she had only paid a married women's stamp – she could not tell her employer she was divorced. "Why?", I asked. "None of their business," she replied, and the subject was closed again.'*

Jess (40)

Rose told us of her anger towards her in-laws who announced they were divorcing a week before her wedding to Nick:

*'The atmosphere was dreadful – my father-in-law was leaving to go off with a close family friend – I was furious they didn't wait until after our day. My mother-in-law was distraught – and was so angry that, in effect, I had to give Nick back to his mother. She certainly needed looking after and that went on for years. Nick got torn in half by it all. Don't tell me adult children don't feel the pain – they do.'*

Rose (39)

# A GOOD WAY AND TIME TO SEPARATE?

Each age – from babies to older children – have their own struggle with grief and loss. It has been said that children are good observers and bad interpreters. Children can observe, and do, more than adults usually realise or acknowledge. Parents are often convinced that children are 'too young' or 'too busy playing' but psychotherapy of both children and adults reveals memories of startling clarity. Often, unfortunately, the children have totally misunderstood what they heard.

*'I remember waking one night and hearing my parents shouting at each other, really shouting. I could hear a word now and again and I heard "Ann" and "I hate Ann". I got up and went downstairs – my mum was actually trying to push my dad out of the house shouting, "go to bloody Ann then"; eventually they saw me and told me to go back to bed. I did, I was only 10. In the morning nothing was mentioned and I didn't dare bring it up. Later, years later, I found out that Dad was having an affair with a girl called Ann, but for a long time I thought it was me they were fighting over and it was all my fault. It also meant I lived with the firm conviction that my parents argued over me, and that my mother hated me. I never referred to it, of course.'*

Ann (18)

Judy described herself aged 7 as, 'a morass of misery'. She used to lie awake and hear her parents shouting at each other in the night. In the mornings – she went on – all would seem to be well and she didn't know what to believe. She could only try to explain the situation to herself by thinking that perhaps she had two sets of parents and this idea became part of her fantasy life. She became very anxious during the day in case the 'other' parents suddenly appeared. It took three years before the situation got so far out of hand that Judy saw her lovely day-time parents' faces contorted with rage. Only then could she begin to understand her observations as her parents explained they could no longer live together because they no longer loved each other. At 10 years old, she found the truth less frightening than her fantasies had been.

*'I can remember an awful silence in the house which went on for weeks – then suddenly we were all called into the kitchen and Mum in tears said to Dad, "Go on tell them." He said he was leaving us, but didn't say why or when he was going. We all just sort of watched him go – my little brother started to cry and my mum said to me you're the man of the family now and something in me froze. We just didn't talk about it. I was nine.'*

Richard

*'I saw my dad packing a case and asked where he was going. I was 7 at the time. He told me Mummy would tell me later and I remember feeling excited because I thought it meant a treat. I never saw him again.'*

Lily (29)

Although the ideal situation might be for a family to sit down and talk about the way the parents can't live together any more, even that they don't love each other, but of course they both love the children, it doesn't always happen that way.

*'I was away at boarding school when my parents broke up so I knew nothing. Suddenly, it was as if my life was on fast-forward – at half-term they weren't speaking to each other and by the holidays he'd gone. I certainly asked "Where's Daddy?", and "Why has he gone?" What I got back was a pained look on my mother's face and a "how could you ask" sigh. In fact my grandmother took me to one side and told me he had gone off with someone and I wasn't to ask*

*my mother because of the upset it caused. I asked her what about me? Doesn't he love me any more either? That seemed to be too much for my grandmother to answer and she started to cry; after that I gave up, I think. A year later my dad came to see me in school and asked how I was. "All right", I replied, and we went out to tea. Nothing else was said. Years later, I asked my father about this and he said he didn't tell me anything because it was self-evident.'*

Gaby (30, and a mother)

We showed Jack our questionnaire. He was 11 when his father left the family. Jack read the questions and his eyes filled with tears.

*'I was all right until I got to question 44 ["Where is Daddy?" and "Is he coming home?"] and in my head I heard myself as a kid asking those questions. I remember doing it and I did get some answers then. Mum did tell me Dad still loved me but I wasn't so sure, and I certainly remember asking if it was something I'd done. I didn't tell anybody at school – I was ashamed I suppose, and that makes me think I did believe it was something I'd done. Perhaps it's different for kids nowadays – I was the only one I knew without a dad at home – it's more common now.'*

Jack (46)

More common now, yes, but each child has to deal with the break-up of their family in their own way.

*'I remember feeling so angry with my parents. I had just gone to university and my parents split up and sold our home within three months. It was as if they had held their breath until I'd gone to Sussex. I was very depressed and wouldn't see either of my parents. Neither came to my graduation. I married soon after and that was a disaster. I have been seeing a therapist for some time now and have come to see that anger can eat you alive if you hang on to it. I am just beginning to see my parents – separately – again. I want Rosie to have grandparents – I feel bad enough she doesn't have a father. I am still confused in my mind over whether my parents were right to*

*stay together, "for the sake of the children". I was the last one to leave home you see; I know now they had been unhappy for years. All I know is that Ben and I broke up when Rosie was a year old. I didn't hesitate. The marriage was a bad one and I didn't want Rosie growing up in a household where you can cut the atmosphere with a knife. I know what it's like. I am truly sorry Rosie doesn't have parents who live together, but at least the situation is an honest one. It was the sham of my childhood I couldn't forgive my parents for – although that's beginning to change through my therapy.'*

Belinda (29, divorced, with one child, 3)

Susan and Jenny were twins:

*'I was always very close to Dad and Jenny to Mum. Dad and I would lark about and play games – Jenny was quieter like Mum. After Dad had gone, my sister and Mum went on being close, but I was really alone. At first we were told he'd gone away to work but somehow it didn't feel right. Jenny seemed OK, but I became quite ill really. I think I hoped if I was really ill Dad would come home – he didn't. Two years later he suddenly rang and asked Mum if we could go and see him. Jenny didn't want to, but I was really excited. I remember going on a train by myself for the first time and he met me in London. The shock was that he was living with someone else and had a baby girl. I don't think I ever got over it. Why wasn't I told? I wasn't prepared in any way. No one told us anything.'*

Susan (12 at time of separation)

An eating problem that began a year later flared into a major eating disorder which lasted throughout her adolescence. Now in her early 20s, Susan is seeing a psychotherapist three times a week and is still struggling to untangle her very mixed feelings about her family.

## 'NOBODY TOLD ME'

In Chapter 2 we heard from women who were very concerned about the effect of a separation on their children and who went to great lengths to listen to the children and to try to answer their questions. Now we are hearing from adults who were children at the time of the break-up and we see a different view: they feel they were not told anything, or not enough. Can this be true?

*'I knew Mum and Dad weren't getting on and when I went on holiday just with Mum, I didn't think anything of it. We went to Scotland and one day Mum pointed and said, "That's your new school." It was the first I knew that we weren't going back home again.'*

Elaine (15 at the time of the separation)

We were fortunate to be able to talk with Elaine's mother. Even after 15 years it was obviously still painful for her to recall that summer and to tell us what she remembered.

*'I remember that year as just so bad – my husband had told me he needed to get away and he made plans to move out into a flat. I couldn't understand what was happening or why; I kept hoping he'd change his mind or I'd wake up from a nightmare.'*

Mrs M (Elaine's mother)

As she struggled to talk to us it became clearer that during this awful time she was not able to think about including Elaine in the planning. There were plans Mrs M didn't want to make, anyway, and part of her probably did want to protect Elaine from the reality of it all. We suggested that she thought that if she didn't put it into words it might not happen? Mrs M agreed that it probably was something along those lines although at the time she doesn't think she thought it out as clearly as that. We did understand that neither parent could or would tell Elaine – perhaps they both hoped the other one would or that somehow she would just know what was going on without being told. In the event, neither did, and Elaine found herself dealing with a succession of massive losses – her father, home, school and friends – without knowing what was going on.

*'I tried to ask Mum questions then but she'd just cry and say, "I don't know." I wrote to my dad and he sent me a postcard saying,*

*"keep on smiling". By the time I saw him at Christmas I thought it best not to ask questions directly.'*

Elaine

Judy remembers her father leaving quite clearly and we have another example of a child well on to the fact that 'something is up' but not asking questions:

*'I was only 8 but I knew something very serious was up, but I didn't know what. I was told, after a bit, that Dad was going abroad to work and he did. I missed him so much.'*

Judy

Judy went on to tell us that her mother re-married and she found herself with a 'smashing step-father'. After some time her father returned to England and he came quite frequently to stay in their house. That is when Judy began to feel quite dreadful. In her words, 'I felt stuck between them.' The worst times were when her father was leaving and Judy would cling to him and cry and then suddenly be aware of the presence of her beloved step-father. She would ask herself whether she was hurting him.

Also, she wanted to call her stepfather, 'Daddy' (especially when a step-sister was born) but she choked on the word and tried 'Pa' but that didn't sound right either. As an adult, Judy marvels over the way the 'grown-ups' seemed to manage the situation. It always seemed civilized and polite and she knows her mother prided herself on the fact there were never, ever, any quarrels. From Judy's perspective the scene was not quite so rosy and she recalls many hours spent in her room privately grieving for her father. Above all, she felt she needed to protect her dear 'Pa' from knowing she missed Daddy very much indeed. The struggle continues as her wedding approaches – can she really be given away by two men? She is certain that she cannot, and will not choose between them.

*'I didn't have to ask, "Where's Daddy?". I knew all along he was going, why he was going, and certainly where. I'd known for some*

*time that he was having an affair. As soon as Mum knew she told me, with all the sordid details. I was 14 and honestly my childhood ended then. My mum had to go out to work full-time and so did I in the sense that I had to look after the boys. I can remember trying to keep everything OK for them. I even told them Dad was away for a bit, and not to be too nosy. How was I to know how to tell them? Mum was too worn out making a living and I resented the chores I had to do. Dad never bothered with us, so these questions about "does he still love us?" don't apply. I knew he didn't.'*

Belinda

## CONCLUSIONS

These stories have emphasised the vulnerability of adolescents when there is a crisis in their parents' marriage. With small children, adults often believe (and hope) that they are too young to understand what is going on; with adolescents, adults often seem to believe (and hope) that they will digest the adult problems while simultaneously dealing with their own task of moving from being a child to an adult.

My advice to another child is "keep out of it."

Age 8
Name James

When Daddy left us me mummy and my sister felt verry sad. Sum times when I was at Daddy's house I some times get a tummy ache.

age 7

I was sad verry sad. I was sick when I was little and Dad lest me.

# Chapter 6
# *Professional Help –*
# *Emotional*

---

*'Hope deferred maketh the heart sick.'*

*Psalm XII*

*'A merry heart doeth good like medicine: but a broken spirit drieth the bones.'*

*Proverbs 17–2*

WE ASKED women who they spoke to about their worries and concerns. Most listed a friend or mother and a small number indicated that they spoke to members of the clergy. If a professional was turned to, however, it was likely to be a counsellor or therapist. In fact, more would have chosen this way if they had known where to find one. This was especially difficult for women not living in one of the major towns, although there are not so many barren areas as there would have been a few years ago. Wherever you are, it can be hard to know how to start getting this kind of professional help.

## COUNSELLING

*'Lots of people told me to get counselling after my marriage broke up, but I didn't know how or if it would cost a lot.'*

Angela

*'I rang around but I just got muddled. I didn't know what kind of help I wanted, I suppose.'*

Laura

89

*'It took me several attempts to find a counsellor who could help me.
I had many desperate moments.'*

Lucy

Some women were unsure whether either a counsellor or
therapist would be the most helpful. Confusion was expressed
about the difference between the two and what help they could offer.

Counselling can be very helpful, especially for someone with a
specific problem. It is not a process which involves looking deeply
into a person's early life but is more likely to be aimed at helping
the client to become more focused on the main issue. It offers
direct support and immediate feedback, sometimes providing
practical advice and other information.

A counsellor may also help the client to explore issues that may
need confronting but be difficult to face. Seeing a counsellor for
even a short time can help someone in the deep distress of a
broken relationship (see Appendix II for details of how to find a
trained counsellor).

A first port of call was frequently Relate (formerly the Marriage
Guidance Council).

*'I attended Relate for five months; it did help.'*

Molly

*'I called Relate but there was a six-month waiting list; I couldn't
wait that long. There was irretrievable marriage breakdown and
lack of will on my part to continue trying.'*

Jenny

*'I knew something was very wrong with my marriage but refused to
believe it could be unresolvable or really serious. I went to see a
marriage guidance counsellor on my own because my husband said
there was no need as he just didn't want to be married any more.
Her first question to me was "Do you think he is seeing someone
else?" Because she put it into words it made me consider it more
seriously and although I said no, it made me go home and look
through my husband's diary and I found proof of his infidelity.
Sometimes you need an outsider for just this extra insight and since*

*it is so completely confidential perhaps one should be more trusting and willing to go.'*

Sandra

One interesting reply to the question 'Did counselling help?' was from Louise, who said that it did but that she didn't think so at the time.

# PSYCHOTHERAPY

Of those women who did find a counsellor, most reported that it had helped and many then went on to therapy later.

Some women who found counselling had helped them to understand more about their present situation, wanted to deepen this understanding and wanted to discover more about why they felt, thought and behaved as they did.

Psychotherapy is about going to the roots of distress, and understanding how past experiences and the way we dealt with them, influence the way we feel and behave today. This involves working with a therapist to look at present and past experiences, and making links between what is in the forefront of your mind and what lies beneath the surface. Anyone who feels stuck in their lives, feels their life has no meaning, or finds themselves repeating destructive patterns can be helped by psychotherapy.

With a counsellor, the immediate problems may have been explored. With psychotherapy, the work takes place much more in the unconscious, and involves looking at dreams, fantasies, thoughts and memories. Therapy is more about exploring the internal world rather than concentrating on external events (see Appendix II for details of how to find a qualified psychotherapist).

*'I worked with a counsellor to help me with my anger and grief over the break-up – it was an essential part of my support network and a lifesaver at the time. Later, I went into therapy to dig deeper into myself to understand more about my part in the choice of partner I'd made. I'd got scared when I'd found myself falling in love again with the same kind of man as my ex.'*

Angela

'I had two failed marriages behind me which left me with a strong wish to understand why my relationships with men started out with such promise and love and ended so painfully for me. In my therapy I spoke at length of my early history and of my relationship with my mother. After some time my therapist told me it was noticeable that there was no mention at all of my father. I see now I brushed off any investigation of why this should be so. I didn't have a father – I replied lightly – he died before I was born. For me at that time, that was the end of that.

As the therapy progressed, it seemed as if that was not entirely so. For the first time, I began to think around the time of my birth and to piece together the facts I had gathered over the years. It became clearer to me that if my father had died one month before I was born, then the effect on my mother must have been catastrophic. Over the years, whenever my mother had spoken about her husband (which she did infrequently) she always called him "my precious", and I began to feel some of the sadness associated with this loss. At the same time, I felt very cheated because after all my mother's "precious" had also been my father.

I dimly remembered asking, "Where's Daddy?", more than once, and the only answer I ever got was couched in terms of my mother's loss. My mother could not understand that I had a claim on him too. I began a journey to find my father, and sought out elderly family members who would have stories and tales about him and I searched for photographs. In therapy I built up inside me a strong picture of my father and, when I could, arranged a collage of photographs and memorabilia. I felt that at last perhaps I knew him, as best I could. With trepidation, I showed this collage to my very elderly mother and waited for a reaction. Mother looked at it in silence for some time and then said, "Fay, your father would have been proud of you." We talked for hours about someone dear to us both – and we could share feelings. My mother was only sad that for so many years she hadn't realised that I truly needed to know my father through her eyes. At 45 years old I feel at last I have had a father and that perhaps my search in both marriages had been for just that – a father – not a husband. It also helped me to make sure that my own daughter kept contact with her father, even though *there were difficulties with the arrangements. I know now how important fathers are.'*

Fay (45, with a daughter, 14)

*'I know it doesn't help the children cope, but it helps me when Mark is not a good father to Ben and John. When he co-operates and buys things and listens to them I feel our happiness is threatened. Do I need therapy?'*

Betty

Betty may be anxious about losing the new family she has created for herself with the boys. The loss of her husband and all those broken promises has made her very wary. We suspect that she gets suspicious when her former husband suddenly keeps to the arrangements they had made. She trusted him once, and she is slowly recovering from the trauma of betrayal. This suspicion does get in the way of her seeing that when her ex-husband is a good father, it actually helps all of them. Therapy? Possibly, but time alone may help to convince Betty about whether or not Bill can really become a good father even though he could not be a good husband to her.

## HELP AS A COUPLE
Some couples do go for help together but for most it seems to be too little, too late.

*'I wish we'd gone to marital counselling before we had major difficulties. Tell other couples to go at the first sign of a problem. By the time we went, it was too late for us.'*

Diana

Some women who answered our questionnaire stayed on seeing the counsellor, even if their partner did not want to continue.

*'Hugh couldn't stand it but I found counselling very helpful. We went to group therapy together, I thought to save our marriage.*

*What happened was we both saw how hopeless it was and Hugh walked out. I stayed with the group to help untangle myself and to work out how to answer some of the questions the children asked.'*
Eve

Eve's use of the word 'untangle' is interesting and useful. Even if the quality of the relationship has been poor for some time, the actual disentanglement can be hard. Not only do the couple have their own situation to deal with but it is complicated by an overlay of feelings (and opinions) of friends and family.

## OTHER SOURCES OF HELP
Advice and support can come from many directions. Women's groups, whether informal or organised, were invaluable. The Church, or Synagogue, were sometimes seen as a source of contact for these groups. Some women we spoke to had contacted the Women's Aid Refuge for advice and help. Health Visitors and GPs may also be able to help. Many more GP practices now have counsellors attached to them and this can be a good place to start.

# Wel-Care
One organisation that specifically helps unsupported mothers is Wel-Care.

*'Twenty years ago I worked for Wel-Care as a social worker and I am happy to say that the climate has changed a great deal since that time. In the 1970s, a pregnant girl on her own received very little sympathy and certainly some men and families "didn't want to know". And this is where Wel-Care came in. There were many Mother and Baby Homes and, at best, they were rather dreary places. But they did provide a roof and one advantage was the help the girls gave to each other. They went into the home six weeks before the baby was due, and if they kept their baby, left six weeks after the birth. In those days there was no, or very little, discussion about the father at all. These were before the days of "birth partners" and the girls were very much alone. A few did have some contact with their baby's father, but he was given no role to*

*play, and certainly not encouraged to visit by the matrons of the Mother and Baby Homes. Public perception has changed over the years and I hear from current social workers that their clients do discuss what to tell the children: "Ought I to be worried that he doesn't know about his father?". Clients do ask for help in explaining to their child about the father who "pops in and out of their lives".'*

Jill

Wel-Care has adapted itself to the changing needs of women as they work with refugees – women who were repeatedly raped and made pregnant, for example. How do you reply to the inevitable questions from children, casualties of war, now on our doorsteps? Or to the questions asked by children about their father, who was last seen taken away by soldiers? Of fathers beaten and tortured in front of their children, and since disappeared? Added to that, there is the loss of their country, home and language.

Certainly, there are still lone mothers who need the support of organisations like Wel-Care. Happily, though, the father's place in the life of the child is given greater prominence in the 1990s than it was in the 1970s.

## ILLNESS – MOTHERS' VIEWS

We were told that although some women did recognise that they needed help, it was not so easy to know what kind and where to turn. We are not clear why so few women were unable to confide in their GP and tell them just what had happened and why the family was so distressed. Can it be that women are still ashamed or embarrassed to tell their doctor about the reason for so much pain in the family? Is there a feeling of humiliation about being left by a man? We cannot believe it is because women do not make the connection between unbearable emotional pain and the body crying out for attention and help. We were told that: 'my son Jack had his first really serious asthma attack a week after we broke up', 'Lily had this tummy ache that went on and on', and 'I saw the doctor because of general poor health, lots of colds, chest infection, eye infection, but I never discussed or mentioned the separation.'

*'I needed a doctor's statement concerning injuries sustained through an attack by my then partner. But the doctor didn't ask to see me again.'*

Carol

*'I thought my GP would see so many cases like mine I didn't feel I could burden him with one more. It was only when I went to the surgery with yet another attack of cystitis and saw a locum – who was a woman – that I started to cry and, oh my, so much poured out. I cried and cried. I think my usual GP had looked too stern and although I know it is silly I thought he'd be cross with me. The woman GP had simply asked me, "What's up?", and to my surprise I sobbed and talked and talked and told her what had happened to us as a family. She sat listening and was very sympathetic. She arranged for me to come to the surgery at the end of her appointments for a weekly talk with her for a bit. I cried a lot, but I had no more cystitis.'*

Jean

Feelings – in adults and in children – if not expressed directly will surface in other ways and they can often affect the body. Many women filling in our questionnaire reported seeing their GP around the time of the separation. Children had tummy aches, sore throats, trouble sleeping . . . whilst the women themselves were more likely to visit their GP because of migraines, weight loss or gain, inability to sleep and depression.

*'When Jacques left me, I hurt – I hurt all over. Every bone in my body hurt. I wasn't quite sure how to describe that to my doctor, so I just told him I couldn't sleep. He didn't ask me if I had any idea why this should be so. I would have liked to have told him, but I couldn't.'*

Anne-Marie

No one should feel that their emotional problems are of no concern to their doctor. In fact, to build up a complete picture of you, a doctor does need to know about major life events. A South London GP confirmed this by saying 'Of course I need to know about such events, even more so when there are children in the family. It helps me to understand otherwise mysterious aches and vague pains.'

# CHILDREN'S INNER AND OUTER PAINS

## Dealing with emotions

Very small children cannot verbalize their feelings, and will therefore 'act out' their stress, often by regressing to an earlier stage in their development. Some of the mothers who answered our questionnaire reported an increase in, for example, bed wetting, or difficulties with their children's behaviour or sleeping patterns which was linked to stress within the family. Slightly older children are more able to speak out – sometimes in an angry or hostile way. It is very important for the child's future mental health that emotions are expressed – even if the things that are said are hurtful or touch on a very sensitive point, although it can be very hurtful to be told by your child 'I hate you' or 'Look what Dad and you have done to me'.

If a parent is feeling fragile or vulnerable, it is hard for them to hold on to being a parent or to listen to the pain expressed by their child. We all experience love and hate towards the same person at different times and as we mature, we find it easier to deal with these ambivalent feelings. If a child is propelled into intense feelings towards one parent with no opportunity to release them, something eventually has to give, and this can be manifested either in a physical or emotional reaction.

'Shortly after my husband left, my seven-year-old daughter developed an irritating cough, which I noticed became worse during periods of high tension between my ex and I. Next she had difficulty with breathing, which developed into a kind of asthma. It was very frightening at night. I was fortunate enough to take Pam to a paediatrician who was also a child psychotherapist and who explained to me some of the underlying psychological causes. He saw it as a reaction to the stress in the family, which was especially high at the weekend, and also an expression of both fear *and anger towards her parents about their break-up. Once I could hear the asthma attack as a cry for help and understand it was Pam's way of showing anxiety, I felt I handled the whole business more calmly, and this did help Pam. Homeopathy helped too.'*

Marcia

Not having the language skills of her older sisters, Pam was left struggling for breath (literally) in order to deal with her strong love for her mother but also her rage at wanting and not wanting to be with her father.

*'I do believe this. I had noticed for a while Pam and I were either so close I could not breathe, or else we were unable to communicate. Rather like my relationship with her father I suppose.'*

Marcia

*'In a child, anxiety may be expressed by the development of certain physical conditions such as asthma, eczema, tummy aches, bed wetting, etc. In the case of asthma, although the susceptibility to it would always be present, problems in the family causing anxiety and grief could precipitate an asthmatic condition. In homeopathic treatment, we would take all these causative factors very much into account when choosing the correct remedy for treating the child with asthma.'*

Dr Adriana Marion (a Homeopathic doctor)

*'I soon connected the children's symptoms with their distress, especially if their feelings got bottled up.'*

Lilly

*'I ask the children at bedtime if they have any problems, and now they know they can talk about anything to me and I will have more time to listen.'*

Julia

*'I think it is important to let the children know you are upset at times. It is OK to cry together and to tell them you are sad and angry too.'*

Carrie

All these women reinforce the value of keeping a space for their children to express their feelings, and therefore to lighten their emotional burden.

## Physical illness

Even illnesses with an obvious physical cause bring the emotional needs of children to the surface:

*'My son John had been ill with chicken pox so instead of my ex husband taking him off for the day, he agreed to come to the house for a few hours to spend time with him. John is always complaining about the travelling to my ex's house so a visit here was what he has always asked for. However, when Pete turned up, after five minutes' chat what does John do? He gets his radio and headphones, puts them on and stays in his own little world.'*

Michelle (mother of John, 7)

*'I think Michelle was lucky. When Phil had a virus and ran a very high temperature I suggested that, instead of going out, his dad came to sit here with Phil. A quarter of an hour later the phone rang again and a rather sheepish voice said on second thoughts he wouldn't come in case he passed on the germs to his new baby. That cheered up Phil no end, I don't think. I was left with a sick child asking why his daddy didn't want to see him.'*

Hannah

What if the children are ill? Should their father be called?

*'A week after David left our daughter had a temperature of 104° one night, I did ring him and he came: we both took her to the hospital. I think now it probably wasn't the right thing to do, but I was scared and it was the first time I had to say, "I'm a lone parent – I have to decide this one." I've got much better at it now, but that first time was so hard. Three years later my daughter still refers to it: "The time I was so ill I had to go to the hospital and Daddy came too, didn't he?"'*

Jenny

*'When Sara broke her arm, I telephoned my ex's office and left a message. Eventually he rang back and asked what did I expect him to do about it? He turned up two days later to see Sara. I suppose better late than never.'*

Betty

Some children are themselves able to make the link between body and feelings. Linda told us that her 5-year-old asked, 'Mummy, when am I next staying the night at Daddy's?' Linda replied, 'On Saturday, darling, that's in three days.' Back came the reply, 'Well, that's why I've got tummy ache then.' Linda said she could hardly believe her ears.

# CONCLUSIONS

In Chapter 1, the pros and cons of talking to friends and family were discussed. Both men and women reported that they often felt their troubles to be a burden on others, and perhaps for this reason alone turned to professional help. Another reason for looking for therapy was more reflective – and came from wanting to know themselves better or to prevent themselves being over-whelmed by feelings of anxiety, confusion or depression.

When looking for help it is essential to find a trained and qualified person (see Appendix II). Counsellors and psychotherapists have different training and the most direct way to find help is to contact an organisation which trains to a high standard.

The second most important point is that when meeting a therapist you should feel comfortable and feel that this is someone you would like to work with, who you can trust, who respects you and what you say, and that this will be treated in confidence. The working relationship between you both will be a very important part of the treatment. Don't be afraid to ask questions at the initial meeting, and be sure to settle important practical details such as fees, frequency of sessions and holidays.

At the time of a crisis we all need someone to talk to, and if you decide to look for professional help of any sort, take your time to find the right person for you. You will be embarking on a very important journey.

WHERE'S DADDY?

# Chapter 7
# *Practical Problems and Professional Help*

'That's the way the money goes'
Pop Goes the Weasel (19th-century song)

## CONSULTING A SOLICITOR

In our questionnaire we asked at what stage a solicitor had been consulted and whether this had been helpful or not. We were told that most women did see a solicitor very early on in the separation.

'Literally five minutes after my father heard that my husband had been having an affair and was leaving me and the children, he was on the phone arranging for me to see a good divorce solicitor. At first this seemed to make the situation terribly "serious" and "public" before I was ready to admit my marriage had failed and I felt the beginnings of an out-of-control situation. Slowly I realised it was the right thing to do, although if it hadn't been for the children I would have liked to bury my head for a few months and hope the situation would just go away. My father was seeing the reality of the situation and I was just putting off the moment of discussions and disclosures of facts, when all I wanted to talk about was my swaying emotions and mixed feelings of shock and disbelief. In a sense, I was waiting for my heart to catch up with my head and to be able to acknowledge that there really was no turning back the clock and the marriage was over.'

Jane

'At the first meeting with my solicitor his opening words to me were that I should not treat him as my best friend or sit there crying for the hour. He not only saved me hundreds of pounds in fees with that advice but also helped me to see exactly what he was there for, and treat my time with him with the seriousness that it warranted.'

Diane

'I had a solicitor who happened to be very human. I felt I was a person, not just a case.'

Gwen

'I was in shock that my husband had left me and Tom for another woman. I opened the Yellow Pages to find a solicitor and I telephoned several before I found one who could see me that day. He had an initial first meeting charge. I was really nervous as it was the first "serious thing" I had done without the support of my husband. I disliked the solicitor at first sight and what he said even more. It was as if he was on the "side" of my husband. He had the cheek to tell me that having an affair was not really so bad and he suggested that I didn't do anything for three months, as in his experience most problems got sorted out and I wouldn't need a solicitor after all.'

Susan

'Seeing a solicitor made the situation more difficult for me because I felt my privacy was being exposed to a complete stranger.'

Elizabeth

This view was echoed by many women but some disagreed:

'We found an inner strength by concentrating on the facts and getting results.'

Rebecca

'The only way to proceed was to remain detached from the emotion of it all anyway.'

Mary

*'I left the divorce proceedings to my husband.'*

Rosa (late 50s)

We found this was often the case in Rosa's generation; perhaps these women had gone straight from their father's home to their husband's, and assumed that their exs' would sort it out for them.

Can it be that in the 90s, when so many marriages are partnerships of equality, that women sought solicitors early on in the separation to give them some weighty backup against their ex-husbands?

*'I needed to get out of my marriage and couldn't do this without the help and advice of my solicitor — my husband was a bully and I was very frightened of him.'*

Jennifer

*Seeing a solicitor made things easier; he was informative and interim maintenance was arranged. I knew where I stood.'*

Lucy

*'Knowing that someone "professional" was acting for me was comforting and reassuring.'*

Jean

*'It made things easier, because then I knew where I stood in the eyes of the law. It raised my hopes of what I could expect financially and backed up my contact ideas.'*

Margaret

This was said many times over, as if the wishes of the mother were not enough without being able to quote the agreement of figures of authority.

*'It made it easier for me to know my legal position, but my husband reacted badly to legal interference. He said that if I carried on with the divorce, he would not continue to see the children, as he*

*couldn't handle a situation like that. I knew that was blackmail but what was I to do?'*

Susan

This was echoed by many women saying that although it made things easier and clearer in their mind, and protected rights, it made any kind of relationship with the children's father much more difficult. None more than Sandy:

*'I felt a lot better having started divorce proceedings; the social worker was glad of course, as my husband had sexually abused the children, but I had some very difficult letters from my husband from the prison.'*

Sandy

*'Things became more difficult because the relationship with my ex deteriorated as he felt threatened.'*

Paula

*'Tim turned into a bully and started saying we should work out our finances together without a solicitor or they would be the only ones left with any money.'*

Mary

*'My husband was a salesman, a very good one, and every time we tried to divide assets, he would make me feel greedy and unreasonable. He tried to come across as a poor man who could barely afford to live – although he managed to pay for a luxurious holiday for him and his mistress in Bali, for pet cats and a dog and more recently, a baby. But if I would only do what he suggested, we would all benefit in the long run!'*

Rachel

*'My husband must be the only man I know who can, because of his gift of the gab, sound like Mr Generous, by suggesting he reduces maintenance or stops paying for one of the children's "extras". Then, after several days of frantic worry, he informs me that "he has*

*sorted it out and things can stay the same after all". He then expects my thanks and a pat on the back.'*

Irene

A solicitor told us that there should be no connection between access and maintenance. If maintenance stops, court applications can be made. A maintenance undertaking is a promise to a court; if someone refuses to honour their undertaking then they are in contempt of court and ultimately could be imprisoned for that contempt.

One other solicitor who we spoke to told us that the Children Act of 1989 encourages parents to make their own decisions about contact with the children of the family. He went on to explain that the court will then only interfere when the parents cannot agree. However, we know from talking to hundreds of parents that this is easier said than done.

*'Seeing a solicitor seemed to ratify a decision after month of doubts and fears.'*

Corinne

*'Seeing a solicitor was essential because he was taking me to court. But I am still trying to get some sort of maintenance from him.'*

Sue

So, seeing a solicitor doesn't mean a passport to success and there are always many factors to be taken into account.

*'My husband paid a derisory £86 per month maintenance for the two boys and he only paid it for eight months. I don't know his current address, so the courts will not do anything about arrears.'*

Jilly

*'When my Dave first went, he told me not only would he pay us maintenance, but that he would always be bringing me things I needed for the house, and give me cash for the children's extras, etc, etc. However, just 11 months after the agreement in court, he*

*suddenly cut maintenance payments without any notification to me and had I ever seen an extra? Oh, no, of course not. His word means as little now as it did throughout the 12-year marriage. A leopard cannot change its spots.'*

Vicki

On the less positive side of seeing a solicitor, some women said it made some things more difficult such as what to do with the house, the car, money and everything else.

*'Seeing a solicitor made everything much more difficult. It caused animosity due to money.'*

Susie

*'Seeing a solicitor made the situation more difficult, because my husband contested the divorce and made outrageous accusations. The reason I left home was he threatened physical violence and to take the children away.'*

Patricia

What if you don't like what your solicitor says? Many women think that once you have contacted one, you are stuck with them. This is not the case: you are paying for the service. Seeing a solicitor can be very daunting and many women, who have to face this technical side on their own, may wish to avoid creating more friction and so opt for the devil they know. Sarah saw four solicitors, each one recommended by a friend, before she found one she felt comfortable with and who seemed able to answer her many questions. She herself had been an accountant for many years before having children and maybe this gave her some assurance to search for the right professional help.

*'Our solicitor made the financial situation clear, but the firm was slow and I had to do most of the work, which meant that my husband and I had to work closely and carefully together.'*

Pat

This seemed to pinpoint yet another problem area: couples who had – for whatever reasons – begun to drift apart, suddenly had to get together to make major decisions.

> 'After spending no time at all alone with my husband for a couple of years, there we were over cups of coffee or glasses of wine hammering out point after point. I did wonder if there would ever have been a divorce at all if we'd spent more time over the previous years discussing details about money and other issues.'

Pat

After all the negotiations, finally getting the divorce can seem lacking in significance.

> 'It took three years of difficult negotiations, unkept promises, hassle and rows, not to mention the letters, telephone calls and money, for Stephen and I to get divorced. When finally the decree absolute came in the post, it was only four typed pages long and didn't seem to be personalised or relevant to me or my feelings. I actually felt nothing. If my solicitor hadn't written me a letter with the decree absolute saying I should keep it in a safe place as it was an important legal document, it would have probably gone in the bin with yesterday's newspapers.'

Jennifer

> 'I received the "absolute" yesterday; it seemed a real anticlimax after two years of grief to get it.'

Fiona

A solicitor's advice can help long after the immediate contact and crisis.

> 'It is now three years since my ex-husband left me and our two small children. I still feel that I need my solicitor behind me, and often telephone him for further advice. My ex-husband was a bully and still is and he periodically reduces the children's maintenance or insists on more contact which he never actually takes up; anything

*to cause me aggravation or grief, partly because I wouldn't take him back after his fling with his secretary.'*

Julie

It is not only the problem of money which can flare up post-divorce and be a problem that requires advice from solicitors.

*'My ex-husband's new girl seems to really resent the contact he has with our children, but now I hear from my son that she has been smacking them. I couldn't bear that, especially as I don't approve of ever smacking children. So I decided to have an off-the-record word with my solicitor, who agreed she had no right to smack my children and it isn't her place to discipline them. He also said that if it happened again I could report it to the relevant authorities, and if it became frequent, her contact with the children could be stopped. I felt so much better after hearing that there was something I could do if it persisted, albeit extreme.'*

Clare

The consensus of opinion was that a solicitor did help even though many women were doubtful at the time.

# FINANCE
The financial struggle between some separated couples was on-going and clearly a major point of conflict.

# *Money*
*'My children were not at all happy with the frequency of visits, but I was afraid to stand up to my husband over this because of the maintenance agreement. I knew if I rocked the boat so would he, financially.'*

Jane

Jane went on to tell us that she had heard somewhere that the word to remember during a divorce is 'parent' and not 'money' but she said it just wasn't possible in her situation, nor in many others.

*'If I tried to discuss money with my ex, he would start to have a go at our access arrangements and want more or less of the children. I knew they were already stressed, and I'd lose the thread of what I was saying. I used to feel confused, although my friends said I was being bullied.'*

Maggie

Paula agreed that money was the real sticking point:

*'I used to think that people got divorced – boom – and then got on with their lives. Little did I know that wrangling over money goes on and on and on.'*

Paula

We were told frequently that being aware of the financial hold that some men had over them affected all aspects of the relationship. In short, some women were afraid to rock the boat too much in case the punishment followed swiftly – as it did for some.

*'I was so badly hurt by William leaving me and the children that I wanted to do something really hurtful back. The trouble is that anything I could do would ultimately hurt the children, so he continued to get away with his bad treatment of me. Also, because he pays us money each month, I feel beholden to him and this adds to my frightened feelings that he will cut off the cash if I show my anger, or am difficult about contact. It is now four years later and I realise that because of the children I can never really be free of him or free to totally run my own life. It is like having a very strict father standing behind me ready to punish me if I don't toe the line. I wish I could be financially independent.'*

Margaret

*'I wasn't working when Jack left and because my youngest was too young for nursery it was not possible for me to get even part-time work. I felt very uncomfortable with the situation since the split, feeling I was getting pocket money from him that was, and at the same time, was not, mine to spend. When he came to pick up the kids, he would notice if I spent money on new clothes or if there was*

*a bottle of wine in the fridge. He would give me hell for being extravagant on his money.'*

Linda

*'I felt guilty every time I needed to spend money on myself as I wasn't working and felt I had to justify all purchases all the time, even basics.'*

Sarah

We were told again and again that men who at first promised to be generous (when feeling guilty) often became resentful and retaliatory later.

*'When my husband walked out on us he said, "I'll be very generous to you and the children." He was feeling guilty at that point I suppose and still tried to look like the good guy. As time went on, though, he tried to backtrack and would plead poverty while taking his new woman off on holiday. Our plans had always been to educate the children privately but once he had a new family "our" plans got shelved. I had to take the kids out of their school and that meant for them the loss of a very stable part of their lives. My head told me to keep the reason for this change of school to myself, but I'm only human and I did let the children know their father wouldn't pay for them any more. I wish it hadn't happened like that. One more of the ideas we had dreamed up together was shattered.'*

Jennifer

*'Our two boys were being educated privately when Ted walked out. He felt pretty guilty at the time and said everything else would stay the same. I'd just about got used to his betrayal of me when he dropped the next bombshell. He said he couldn't pay school fees any longer – stopped just like that. Ted told me to mortgage the house I had received as a settlement. I told him he must be crazy if he thought I would jeopardise any of the security we did have. And how would I pay it back? I could lose everything. It was typical of his way of thinking: "Get what you can today, pay for it later if you can." To take the boys out of school was the cruellest of blows – I*

*can't forgive him for that, but he was involved with another woman
and also had a baby to support.'*

Camilla

Rosemary, whose husband died, found people were more helpful about financial worries:

*'My son was immediately offered a bursary by his school when his
father died: they were very sympathetic to my sudden financial
worries.'*

Rosemary

In Chapter 11 we look in more detail at losing a husband
through death. What is markedly different and immediately
noticeable is the level of compassion shown to a widow, whereas
women who are on their own because of a split in the relationship
are less likely to receive unconditional sympathy and support.

*'I became frightened and worried that if I argued he would go
further and cut the maintenance he provided for the children. Paul
asked me accusingly one day, "Are you saying it's Daddy's fault
that I can't have crisps for my school break any more?" It is so hard
to explain that there is just less money for everything and everyone
now.'*

Camilla

*'When Jack left me and the kids, he took the car with him as he
needed it for work. So life is harder for us on a practical level as we
have to go everywhere by bus and the kids hate walking far in the
rain. Shopping I have to do with a neighbour as we are so far from
the supermarket. I hate the way it makes me feel a nuisance by
asking continually and I am an ongoing burden to my friends. Now
on contact days the kids think it's brilliant to go with Dad in the car
everywhere and I feel resentful of this and angry that Jack has in
effect clipped my wings at the same time as forcing me to be more
independent.'*

Linda

'My alimony only lasted four years as my ex-husband hated paying and I'd do anything for a quiet life.'

Mandy

'I'm still trying very hard to get some through the Child Support Agency. I thought they were supposed to chase the father and get money for us.'

Kathi

'Money was very tight when Mike left us. I would go wild with rage when I would be struggling to buy the kids some clothes they really needed and he would take them out and buy them some ridiculous, unnecessary clothes or toys. I used to beg him to ask me what they "needed" if he was going to buy anything. But no, that wasn't his style. Rowing about money certainly cast a shadow over changeover times and that was very hard on the kids; in fact I think it was during handover they heard us row the most.'

Pat

'When the kids' father came to collect them, I used to feel they were being cut in half. It is at the point of changeover that it really hits one that it is the children who are suffering, especially if these are rows about money, and I'm afraid there were, frequently.'

Jane

'When Pete left me and the twins we had to sell the house immediately because Pete also lost his job. I bought a small flat on the other side of town with my half of the proceeds. Six months and a lot of travelling later, Pete turned up again and said he wanted half of my flat as he was penniless. I was distraught.'

Audrey

'Jonathan walked out on us and moved in to the house of his well-off girlfriend. For the first year after he went, there were no changes to my own and the children's financial situation or any noticeable changes to our lifestyle. When I forced the situation to change by seeing a solicitor and started divorce proceedings, he was amazingly *fair and arranged for a very generous settlement and maintenance. I know when I hear from my friends in similar situations that I am very lucky that there is more than enough money which means there is no real fighting to do. We can concentrate on the children and feel that we both can give the best to them. It's not that money is everything but it surely helps.'*

Sandra

*'I told the Child Support Agency who the father of my boy is and they called him in for an interview. He admitted he was the father and signed the form. A few months later he asked for a review and denied paternity. I wondered how much more I could take. The CSA didn't believe him as he had signed and he still has to pay maintenance. I was believed.'*

Carol

*'Financially, the future scares me. We are in rented accommodation. I have no private pension or savings.'*

Brenda

*'I only have a very small professional pension as I was only ten years in full employment.'*

Lucy

*'It is hard when your ex-husband turns up on contact days wearing new clothes and with a sun tan, when you are struggling to make ends meet. My parents try to help, but they're on a pension.'*

Liza

*'For me there was no maintenance – my husband returned to training and I would have had to maintain him if I had pressed the case.'*

Amy

## Property

When something as dramatic as a separation happens, the last thing you need is the major stress of moving house. But in reality this is often what happens, so the children may have to start at new schools and lose their friends and familiar surroundings all at once.

> *'Moving house is a jolly expensive business, and the stress was terrible. We all hated to lose our home and I'll never forgive my ex-partner for that.'*
>
> Jenny

> *'I worried about the money side of moving, especially as I didn't want to move to a flat, who would? But I have to say that the problems I encountered over it were something I could share with other people, and that they could understand and help me with. It is always so much easier to talk about practical worries than emotional ones.'*
>
> Rebecca

> *'When Jim left he told me he would not pay the mortgage on our house, and he didn't. The only thing we could do at the time was to move away to my sister's home. Perhaps we should have stayed put but I didn't and anyway what good would a huge debt hanging over us have done? But the kids lost a lot that summer, more than just a house.'*
>
> Marie

## Pensions and benefits

A pension bill currently going through Parliament will, when enacted, allow pension rights to be split on retirement. The lobby pressing for a 'clean break' would enable pension rights to be split at the time of divorce rather than at retirement.

> *'The first shock I had was hearing that I had lost a legal entitlement to a share of my ex-husband's pension. The second shock was to be told I had lost my rights to any benefits from his state pension too. Tell anyone just divorcing to plan for their retirement now, before it's too late.'*
>
> Beryl

If one parent leaves the family, the other is entitled to One-Parent Benefit, regardless of income, in addition to child benefit. If the mother works over 16 hours a week she may be able to claim for Family Credit. If not working, or working less than 16 hours per week, then Income Support can be claimed. When Family Credit or Income Support is applied for, the Child Support Agency will become involved in an effort to claim this money back from the father. A useful leaflet FB2 can be obtained from Department of Social Security offices.

# MEDIATION

Mediation is often seen as a civilized way of dealing with difficulties. There is a growing awareness that this service exists and is available to help parents iron out problems in a reasonable way. Mediation is about agreeing on access arrangements for the children and how property is to be divided.

Couples can speak directly to each other, rather than through intermediaries and in the best of all possible worlds (and divorces) agreement is reached on highly charged emotional issues. It is hoped that mediation reduces hostility between the partners and, by fostering direct communication, encourages cooperation. The aim is to help parents find their own solutions, and a more flexible attitude can mean it is possible for a couple to return to re-evaluate their agreement if new situations arise.

The Children Act recognises that family life has changed in Britain. One alteration is to give unmarried fathers legal status if the parents register joint parental responsibility for their children. The key words in the Act are 'parent' and 'joint responsibility' for children, even if the parents' own relationship has ended. In our discussions with women and men we were informed again and again that mediation (and solicitors) encouraged them to make arrangements for their children without having decisions forced on them by the courts. Old words like custody, care and control have been superseded by terms such as parental responsibility and contact.

*'My ex-husband had to learn that parental responsibility means acting responsibly. It was a hard and difficult lesson for him.'*

Marge

Working with a mediator is far cheaper than corresponding through solicitors or going to court. Mediators are not interested in the past, which some women found hard to bear. Their sole interest is the future, particularly the future of the children. The mediation service speaks directly to the couple as parents, not as man and wife.

*'Agreement is reached by forced compromise as mediators are there to make it right for the sake of the children regardless of parental differences.'*

June

Mediation is not about the possibility of saving a marriage. Mediation is not therapy, and should not be seen as such – it is not about feelings, but about what should be done or not done. Neither will it be successful if both parties are not willing to be open to compromise. There are few perfect solutions and quite often it is about agreeing on the least painful of all options on offer. This is not a time for emotional reactions but for careful and logical thought.

*'I was really nervous of going because I was so unconfident in myself, and my ex-husband was such a good talker. I felt at a disadvantage knowing he could twist everything I said to make it sound so unreasonable. In the event he 'blew it' by saying that he wanted the children to stay the night with him so that he could discipline them. That went down like a lead balloon.'*

Carol

*'I went to the mediation meeting prepared with a list of examples why Jim was a poor father who was pushing for more contact for the wrong reasons, but the women were not interested in the past, only*

*the future and that we both should leave the room having signed the contact agreement paper.'*

June

*'When we went to mediation I tried to think with my head, but my heart still said punish him. Mediation did help me to see that by punishing him sometimes I was punishing the children too, and I didn't want to do that.'*

Diana

*'My man and I couldn't work the contact out between ourselves at all because the children insisted they didn't want to go and see him when they could be playing with their friends instead. He had walked out on them after terrorising them all their lives, and they just wanted to start enjoying a peaceful life without him. The mediators said they should go to him one weekend day a week. They refused, and I wouldn't make them, so we had to go to court, but my ex didn't turn up, and so it is still going on. I think the mediators are a lot of middle-class women poking their noses into other people's business. I bet they don't even have kids themselves.'*

Sue

Not all women felt so angry.

*'They were a great help to me and Matt because they made us realise that when the children were with one parent, the other one had to let go and accept that things might not be to their liking, but that was life. Also we did compromise with the contact so that we both felt we got most of what we wished for. Not ideal but certainly a better arrangement than the mess we had been in.'*

Lily

Our most frequent answer to the question, 'Did you see a mediator?' was 'no'.

*'It had gone too far, there were too many lies.'*

June

*'We did not feel it was necessary.'*

Mary

*'We did not think about it; we had a natural instinct not to talk to an outsider.'*

Paula

*'We both thought the relationship was already over. I was muddled, I thought it would be about reconciliation.'*

Sue

We got the feeling that a great many more women would have liked to give mediation a try but their partners were not interested.

*'My partner was not really interested, so I didn't try either.'*

Sandra

*'I went alone; he refused to.'*

Irene

One interesting reply to the question, 'Did mediation help?' was Louise's:

*'Yes it did, but Harold didn't think so. He felt told off.'*

Louise

*'I got confused. I thought conciliation meant reconciliation. I found my way to a mediator and it did help us in several ways; we straightened out some problems we couldn't agree on. I'm glad we went.'*

Jenny

# CONTACT CENTRES

Over the past nine years, more then 100 contact centres have been opened in England, Wales and Scotland. None are funded by the government.

The Coram Meeting Place in London is a neutral venue for professionally supervised children's contact. It provides a setting for contact visits in an atmosphere similar to an out-of-school play area. This centre is run in partnership with the Inner London Probation Service – others are run by Churches or the WRVS. It is hoped that these kind of contact centres will find demand increases for their services. The hope is that contact can be arranged between the non-resident parent and child in a situation in cases, where for a variety of reasons, the parents have been unable or unwilling to arrange this themselves.

The reasons for this are often complex, but violence or allegations of abuse may be an issue. In these instances the resident parent may be unwilling to let the other parent take the child out of the building. Fear of abduction is frequently cited. However, we are told that after a few visits parents can usually come to a more private arrangement. Parents who do not wish to meet face-to-face can make arrangements to use separate waiting rooms.

Information can be hard to find, but it is worth trying the Coram Foundation. A spokeswoman said, 'The child is the focus of our concern and we aim to provide a service which helps parents and carers to protect and enhance children's well-being.' In 1994–95 they arranged contact for 118 children of 81 families and supervised 589 visits.

What of the families who use these facilities?

*'I turned up at a contact centre because I had no choice, I had vowed never to see Lee again and I meant it. He had almost killed me on many occasions before the matter was taken out of my hands and Pete and I were able to leave. However, I was able to arrange that Lee was never going to see Pete alone in case he started taking his aggression out on him. The women at the centre welcomed us and took Pete into another room where Lee was waiting. I've decided to put up with this situation because I know it won't be long before Lee finds another victim and then will probably lose interest in Pete. Pete quite likes coming here because he says he feels safe with his dad, unlike the past years at home. These visits are only two hours and he likes playing with the other kids there and eating the sweets Lee brings.'*

Maggie

Fiona works as a volunteer at a North London Contact centre and witnessed a mother turn up at her centre recently and hand over her son, saying she was off to the library while her son and ex spent a day together. The mother was red in the face and most indignant to have to be in the centre at all, telling anyone who was in earshot that her ex had not seen her son since he was first born. Fiona took the 8-year-old boy through to where his dad was waiting with a box of toys, books and clothes as a late Christmas/welcome present. Fiona said she almost cried watching the sheer pleasure and unspoken joy on both their faces and wondered what situation had caused them to have missed out on so much time together.

# CHANGES IN LEGISLATION

A lot of media space was given to the Lord Chancellor's proposals for radical reform, legislating that all couples will have to face a panel of legal and other experts before being allowed to proceed with a divorce. Couples would be fully informed about conciliation services, marriage guidance and whether lawyers should be consulted. Couples would also be told about the Child Support Agency.

Whether or not these reforms have been attempted to offset the tremendous financial cost of matrimonial legal aid (rather than the emotional costs) is uncertain. A Parliamentary bill is expected to follow requiring divorcing couples to use professional help to deal with the aftermath of break-up.

The Lord Chancellor is convinced that the current law inflicts unnecessary damage on children and that these reforms would help divorcing parents to think about the welfare of the children instead of becoming embroiled in battles and blame. The children must come first and satisfactory arrangements for them must be made.

However, these proposed reforms have not gone forward as smoothly as predicted. The Law Society has spoken out in opposition to these changes and their fear is that the proposals will 'invade the privacy of those whose marriages break down'. The main thrust of the proposals to remove fault from the divorce process is supported by the Society. Couples would be able to obtain a divorce after a 12 month cooling-off period to give time for arrangements over children and finances to be sorted out. But the Law Society foresee that the changes would still fail to meet the needs of those using the proposed system. They have reservations about the plan to encourage more people to settle differences with the help of trained mediators rather than in court: 'Some people could accept less than they are entitled to.'

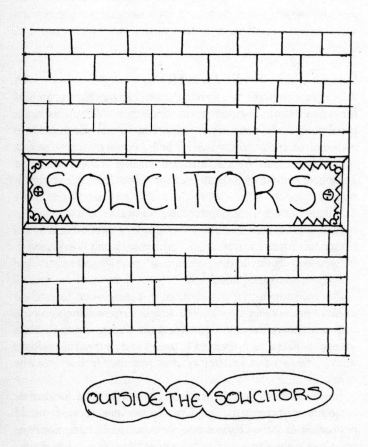

OUTSIDE THE SOLICITORS

# Chapter 8
# *Further Support*

'The best gift a man can give his children is to love
their mother.'

Hoarding, Los Angeles

## GRANDPARENTS

When marital problems arise, each set of in-laws may side with
their own son or daughter. When a family is under the strain of
deciding whether to dissolve or to maintain an unhappy marriage,
grandparents can be very important to the children, particularly in
providing a constant presence. The relationship for a child with a
grandparent is always significant and can help to foster in a child
a deep sense of family belonging. For some children the grandparents can make excellent parental substitutes, especially if they
live close by or the mother has to work.

*'My daughter Beryl came back home to live when she was pregnant.
I never knew who the father was and when Charles was born Beryl
was very vague and uncaring. In fact, after a few years she went off
with someone else. My heart was in my mouth until she said she
didn't want to take Charles, and Charles certainly didn't want to
leave me or my husband. We settled down to being full-time parents
again and Beryl has little to do with us. You try answering questions
like, "Where's Daddy?" to a little boy when you have no idea who
or where he is. How do you answer questions like, "Doesn't he love
me?". All this happened years ago, but I still am weeping inside
remembering how many times Charles asked these questions and I
struggled to answer. Even now he's a man he feels it. Last week he
was playing tennis and a friend said how good he was: "Do you take*

*after your father?" How is Charles to know? – so many questions, so few answers.'*

Joan

For a boy with an absent father the relationship with a grandfather can be central to his development as he sees him as a role model and copies his masculine attitudes.

*'I retired and I must admit to the joy of helping to bring up my two grandsons. I have time with them and for them I never had with my own children – I was too busy making a living.'*

Gordon

Grandparents can be especially supportive to a daughter left to care for children – they can be helpful all round. However, the children must be in no doubt that it is their mother who still has prime care and ultimate responsibility for them. No-one must lose sight of the fact that the mother and child bond is the strongest and must be maintained. If there are conflicts, the children must be protected. Otherwise, divided loyalties will confuse them more.

Lily told us that she had never got on very well with her mother and her dad had died two years previously. Lily did return home with her daughter – she was driven to this because of desperate financial worries:

*'My mum just took over, and I felt about 15 years old again. All our old conflicts flared up and I began to feel surly and miserable. I went to see a counsellor who helped me in many ways but specially to know the difference between being a daughter, wife and mother. I wished I'd seen her 10 years ago.'*

Lily

Ideally, parents can see their own parents as a crucial source of emotional gratification for their children. Some grandparents have the interest and desire to provide their grandchildren with love, time and affection – the most effective way of preventing any harmful psychological effects of separation or divorce.

'When my daughter found her circumstances had changed radically and she was a one-parent family she asked if she could come to stay with me with the children most weekends and holidays. As a widow I was delighted, but I realised there had to be some changes. Up until then I had been a fun-gran and enjoyed seeing them pretty regularly to go to the fair or cinema. Now I realised the boys were going to be living in an all-female environment and perhaps I should take on a slightly different role. Whereas previously the boys had parents to discipline them, there was now only my daughter. My ex-son-in-law had opted out entirely. I felt I should become a back-up for my daughter and instead of being the one to ask for bedtime to be stretched I should, now and again, be the one to call time, or to remind them of their manners. Otherwise it seemed so unfair on my daughter for her to be the only one who said no to the children.'

Doris

'One thing I could not understand was that although the children were fussing about staying overnight with their father and his wife, they often begged to be able to stay at their grandparents' house. Why was that?'

Debbie

Could it be that there was no pressure on them to go, that they had a choice in the matter or that there was no tension during handover created by either adults or children? Maybe it was because staying the night at their grandparents' house would be natural and not forced; also they were safe in their knowledge that they would be back with their mother the next day. We felt this touched the very core of their security. It is very sad when children do not have deep-down trust with the non-custody parent because of the range of feelings they have about being left.

'My husband became very moody and bad-tempered. I thought he was having a breakdown and I asked his parents to come and stay and they did. They were worried about him too, and helped to look after the children one weekend to give us time on our own to talk.

*They told me not to worry. Once the truth hit us and we knew he was involved with someone else and planned to leave me and the children, my in-laws stopped seeing me. Six weeks later they had my husband, his new woman and our children to stay over Christmas in their house. I was appalled because there was no prior discussion or warning for the children, and they suffered a great deal, this being the first time they slept away from me. To be faced with meeting their father's new girlfriend at such a delicate time was a shock which they coped badly with and they regressed sorrowfully. I myself was very hurt, for different reasons of emotional betrayal. I couldn't believe it after the initial support I had been shown, when the reason for the marriage hiccup had been put down to ill health and overwork. Blood is thicker than water I suppose, and always will be.'*

Patsy

Most of the comments we received about in-laws showed that few kept in touch with their spouse's family. Even if there was initial contact, it seemed to fade out. This perhaps was difficult for the children – for younger children it would divide their families right down the middle. If this happened it is helpful for one set of grandparents to mention the other in a favourable way to let the children know they can talk to one set about the other.

*'My daughter said when I mentioned her father's brother, "Oh, do you know him, then?" She was too young to remember I'd known him as long as I had her father, I just hadn't seen him since the break-up.'*

Melissa (mother of daughter, 4)

*'When Dad left us I remember he used to take me to see his mum and dad about twice a year. They were kind, but I never really got to know them. I saw my mum's family all the time – they are my real family.'*

Judy

The essential point is to try to let grandparents know how you would like some questions answered if they crop up. It does not help the children if any bitterness shows through, if, for example, feelings about an abandoned daughter filter through to the children.

*'My gran was very wise. I used to ask her all kinds of things I wouldn't ask my parents. I always felt there was a cover-up going on with them, but I trusted my gran.'*

Jennifer

*'My Granny helped me a lot – she made it possible for me to understand that my mother had divorced only my father – neither had divorced me. I did still have two parents. I also felt safer knowing she was there to look after me if anything happened to them both.'*

Philippa

*'I always felt good at my grandparents – both lots, but when we were at my mother's parents I had the best time. Mum was more relaxed and I recall feeling very safe there.'*

Penny

The word security was often used in relation to grandparents. It is a vital ingredient of a child's mental health and an aid to their future view of relationships. Whether consciously or unconsciously, children of divorced parents often come to regard human relationships as basically unstable, and a solid relationship with a grandparent can help to correct this idea.

When Beverly said to her 6-year-old daughter that she expected that she would go and live with her father if anything happened to her the reply came:

*'No, no, no, I never will ever go and live with Daddy and Sandy. I'd go and live at Grandma's and Gramps – I would have your old bedroom and that room by the kitchen could be my playroom.'*

Lee

In fact the whole extended family (for those lucky enough to have one) takes on an added importance. The constancy and stability it offers becomes an internalised security. It helps us to feel safe deep inside ourselves and this can help to minimise the fear of being rejected again, which otherwise can linger into adulthood and affect future relationships. It is easier for a child within the context of a loving family to find a way to cope with loving two people who do not now love each other.

*'I found it hard to convince my granddaughter that none of us would stop loving her, whatever happened. I was so upset when she said to me, "Mum and Dad promised to love each other when they got married, but now they don't." I am sure her demanding behaviour was just a way of checking us out, but she was difficult, and it was not easy to stay sympathetic when she was so rude, it's all been so awful.'*

Heather

*'When my daughter and son-in-law were going through a very rough patch in their marriage, I took Caroline to the theatre to see The Patchwork Quilt. What I didn't realise was that the sub-plot was about a girl living only with her mother. In the play, one day, the girl starts to ask, "Where's Daddy?", and accuses her mother of keeping her father away from her. Eventually the girl in the play solves the problem by spending time with each and at the end reunites her parents.*

*As we left the theatre I could see Caroline was very tense and I thought it time for a Coke, and perhaps a chat. We talked about The Patchwork Quilt for a bit and then Caroline said, 'Oh Grandma, don't let's talk about the little girl who had to choose between her Mummy and Daddy.' I longed to find some wise words to help Caroline, but I didn't know what to say to her. What I did later was to tell my son-in-law and daughter in no uncertain way just how worried their daughter was and to get their act together, and for heaven's sake tell Caroline something. I know that did sober them and they faced up to whatever their problems were and went to Relate. Without witnessing Caroline's distress, I would never have*

128

*dared speak to them about something I considered a private matter – but seeing her little face made me bold. They all seem happy enough now. It's not easy being a grandmother and mother-in-law.'*
Deborah (grandmother of Caroline, 8)

We cannot stress strongly enough the importance for children of all ages to have good experiences of relationships with other adults with whom they can form strong emotional bonds. If grandparents are available and willing, see them as a blessing whether they are your parents or not.

*'Mummy, I know that you will never leave me, but if you did who would I live with, Grandma or Aunty Joan? I can't make my mind up because they are both so nice.'*
Tammy, 5

It didn't occur to her she would go to her father.

*'I went to see my parents a lot during the time of my divorce – I felt there I could share the responsibility of care of the children even if just over-night. I know, too, that my parents gave the girls a bit of space if they wanted to talk about the situation at home. I'd clear out of the way and give the girls time to be alone with my mother and father. I had had a long discussion at the beginning with them and although at first we did wonder what to tell the children about certain aspects of the separation we worked out a possible blue print of answers. We wanted to be sure we all kept to the same kind of explanations so they wouldn't become more confused.'*
Jennifer

Angela told us that her parents had died several years earlier and she felt their absence acutely when her marriage ended. She felt very alone. Angela said she tried to keep in contact with her ex-in-laws both for her own sake and for the children, but she noticed their welcome became less warm when her ex-husband became involved with someone else. Her advice is to 'find "grandparents" wherever you can – look around the neighbourhood – borrow other people's – look for a grandmother when looking for a baby-sitter, but find them.'

> 'Three years after the separation from my husband, the children and I went to stay with some new friends who turned out to live in the same village as my ex-in-laws. I said to the children on the journey, "Shall we pop in to see your nanny and grandpa for a few minutes as they live here too?" My daughter said yes but my son said no because, I think, he was more aware of the possible difficulties of the meeting (after all I hadn't seen them for over two years). We rang the bell and the look on my ex mother-in-law's face said it all. There was an open look of delight, pleasure and surprise, almost gratitude, on her face as she hugged and kissed us all. We stayed half an hour and the children at first were clinging to me as if to stay close until they knew I was OK. After we left my son said, "They really do still love you don't they or they wouldn't have kissed you so much." After the visit, the children were really happy and said "that was nice wasn't it?" and were quite excitable. In a way I felt it was a visit long overdue and that the children had really benefited from this single act, one which I had not been ready to face before.'
>
> Suzanne (mother of daughter, 3 and son, 8)

The 1989 Children Act acknowledges the importance of children's relationships with all family members. However, grandparents have not been placed in a special category. A judgement given on 30 April 1995 was that 'a grandmother did not have the automatic right to apply for contact with her grandchildren who had been placed in care but had to seek the leave of the court so to apply'. Grandparents are not given preferential treatment and need to apply for leave for contact orders or a residence order. But when looking at all the uncertainties it is still clear that the court has regard for the nature of the contact and the more meaningful and important the connection was to the child, the greater the weight that would be given. Thankfully, contact between a child and family was assumed to be beneficial.

# THE SCHOOL

We feel it is very important for all the carers in a child's life to be kept informed about the changes at home, and we were told repeatedly how helpful teachers were.

However, some mothers' stories were not so happy:

*'At one time my daughter Kate was having difficulty being left by me at school. She would cling to me and cry; the more distressed she got, the more helpless I felt. Her teacher grabbed Kate from me and told me to go. She told me later Kate was "fine" after 10 minutes, but at what inner cost? The advice was "just leave her quickly and she'll be OK," but I had to cope with her being dragged off by her father every contact day and I wasn't going to have her wrenched from me on a daily basis by her teacher also and I had to tell the school this. It wasn't easy.'*

Lorna (mother of Kate, 6)

*'I had a talk with my son's teacher and kept her fully informed about our situation. I was very upset when just before Christmas the class made cards and Andrew, only five years old, was told to write "to Mum and Dad with love". He was very tearful that evening and told me about it. It was even worse when he brought it home because he said he didn't know who to give it to. I went back to the school, because I knew for a fact there were at least three other children in the class who did not live with both parents. It was all so uncaring and thoughtless. I did make a fuss although it was too late to help Andrew and I had to deal with that – but I hoped it would make the teachers involved think more carefully next time.'*

Tracy

A very sensitive way of a teacher dealing with an issue of one-parent-families, was related by one mother:

*'When my daughter, who is six, brought back her homework which was to draw around one foot of everyone who is in the family, the note from the teacher also said "Don't worry if some members of*

131

*your family are not at home." That really eased a possible tricky
situation.'*

Paula

If a child is finding the handover difficult or is tired after a
weekend travelling between parents, then the school should know
about this. Some parents – initially – feel reluctant to reveal details
of the family's private affairs to a stranger. Again, we were told of
women holding back on telling outsiders in case their husband
returned. However, for a child, an absent father, even in a trial
separation, is hard to deal with and the child will need all the
support and understanding available. It is wise, if at all possible, to
tell the teacher before a separation because a caring teacher can in
many ways make sure the child is happily busy and be on hand to
provide support, advice and reassurance.

*'I feel we all received so much help from Beth's teacher. She knew
Beth (who is 6) was having problems moving between her dad and
me and sometimes on a Monday would send home with her a little
note telling me how Beth had been in school that day.'*

Jackie

*'My daughter, 7, started falling behind at her new school. I went to
see her teacher, and she said to me that Jenny had missed some very
basic learning skills which she should have learnt two years ago. I
realised that although Jenny had been to school, she had had too
much on her mind to concentrate. And I'd had too much on my
mind with the divorce, to notice. Her teacher and I worked out a
plan to help Jenny catch up on the work she'd missed.'*

Joy

*'In my class Bob, 8, started being cheeky and disruptive and his
work started to fall off. Later we discovered that was when his father
started abusing him sexually. His father went to prison and Bob was
told that. Once it was out in the open I felt I could help.'*

Hazel (an infant teacher)

Claudia, also an infant teacher and not a parent, contacted us because, she said:

> *'I see the results. I have children in my class with tremendous difficulty in accepting the situation, and their part in it. They become unable to concentrate on work that they had previously been enjoying.'*
>
> Claudia

She continued by saying that she did not know how to help and was unsure whether to say that things will get better or just to give them hugs and attention. Her experiences led her to believe that parents get caught up in their problems and do not recognise that those around them have problems too. Claudia says she does not need to know everything, but does need to be kept in the picture. Then she can take the necessary steps to help the children in her class to cope with the situation as well as possible.

# AU PAIRS AND OTHER DOMESTIC HELP

Mothers who had au pairs or nannies were fortunate to have extra support both for the child and for themselves. It is not an easy position to be in, we were told, witnessing the pain of a family at close quarters, especially if you are living in the house.

Libby (now in her 20s) told us about her nanny. When her parents began to scream and shout at each other her beloved nanny could no longer stand the strained atmosphere and left after looking after her for 5 of her 7 years. Three months later, her father too left the home for good and Libby said for her the sun went out and everything seemed grey for years. It is only now that Libby is in therapy that she can understand how depressed she was as a child and how such major losses and changes affected her life so deeply. She can recall quite vividly 'before' and 'after' the losses of her nanny and father, although in her memory now the pain over her father and nanny tend to merge in to one. A much loved step-father came on the scene and that eventually helped to some extent. Libby said with him she could become cheerful on the outside again, but not inside – that was still grey.

*'When my partner left us, I had to find a job quickly. First I had to find someone to look after my three small children. I tried "word-of-mouth" child minders but didn't feel happy with any of them. I moved the kids around a lot. I tried a student who swapped accommodation for child care and that didn't work out either. Two sacked au pairs later, I realised I was looking for the impossible – a real partner to share the responsibility of the three kids under five years. I gave up the idea of work and now live on state benefits.'*

Connie

Sandy was nanny to two little boys of 3 and 4. It was her first job. She told us how shocked she was when the mother told her the father had gone off.

*'I talked to the mother's mother and my parents about what was happening because I didn't feel mature enough at 18 to deal with what was going on. The children at first were very quiet and not their usual bouncy characters. Then, as the weeks passed, the older boy started having angry outbursts and I felt he needed a father figure around. The little boy regressed badly; he became clingy to me and his mother and was very easily upset. There were no changes in a practical sense but a lot emotionally. I always told the mother anything the children asked or said as I felt she should know and I needed help to answer the questions, it was best that we should answer the same. The children did not want to see their dad and were angry, even for such small children. They often said they hated him, and why did they have to see him. I felt that as he had not been there very much during the week and had not regularly bathed the children or put them to bed, they were very much in the same routine as they were used to but knew things were never going to be the same again. They would alternate between saying they hated me (probably because I was there and their dad wasn't) and asking me if I was going to leave them too. I spent so much time*

*wanting to cry myself at the loss of this family unit and of the difficult time ahead for them all.'*

Sandy

*'I was left very suddenly by my boyfriend when Julie was only eighteen months old. I was desperate. I had to work and left Julie two days a week with one baby minder and the other three days with different friends who would help out. Eventually I got a nursery place for her but not before she suffered a lot from all the change in her life.'*

Molly

LouLou, a more mature nanny of three children, felt that for the first few weeks she was nanny to four, as the mother was not able to organise anything.

*'I felt it was my duty to keep things in the house as much the same as usual. My hours increased plus I had to do shopping and cooking as well as give the family emotional support. I was 24 and in a way I enjoyed the responsibility and challenge of running a family. My fiancé and I decided that we were ready for a full commitment and set the date for our wedding and by the time the family was back on its feet, I was married and expecting my own child.'*

LouLou

Both these nannies answered the questions from the children with positive words such as, 'Daddy loves you very much and will see you soon.'

All the nannies of small children commented on how fractious the children became when the absent parent came to visit.

*'When the children came home from a visit they needed a lot of calming down.'*

Honor

One au pair who talked to us remembers the strain of trying to get the children out of the room when the parents began to quarrel.

135

*'I was only very young myself and had very little English to help the children. They would cry and I would physically comfort them, but could not explain and I know their mother and father did not tell us what was going on. When I went home for Christmas I just did not go back. I felt bad for the children but as I said, I was young, and it was too much for me at that time.'*

Denise (17)

*'I was au pair for a very nice family, then suddenly there was a terrible atmosphere and the mother was very tearful and irritable. No-one told me what was going on; at first I thought it was something I had done. The children began to misbehave and became very disruptive. I did not know what to do. I did ask the lady but she wouldn't say, and even after the father packed up and left she still did not tell me or the children he had gone. She told friends that he was working away from home, but I knew that was not true. I felt very sad for the children but as they were worried about their father's absence their behaviour got worse and I left. I cried when I went − it was very sad.'*

Marie (18)

One nanny replied to our question about whether there were any changes in help with the children by saying, 'Yes, I got the sack.' She told us that the whole family went away for a holiday and while in Spain the father had to return to England 'on business'. A few days later the mother took Tricia (the nanny) into her confidence and said she believed that her husband had gone to be with someone else. Later that day she flew home leaving Tricia to bring the children home at the end of the week. By the time they returned the fat was truly in the fire and the parents had split up. Tricia said her employer decided to take the children to her mother's and as finance was one of the major battles Tricia should look for another job at once. Not at any time, she says, were the needs of the children considered and although the boys were 4 and 6, neither parents explained to them what was really happening. Tricia had no further contact with the family.

In one particularly complicated situation, Diana's husband had left home to set up house with the then au pair. Diana had two children (a girl of 7 and a boy of 9) and had difficulty in coping with the double betrayal. Diana's account of her family's break-up included telling us of the problems her children had in seeing Inga, especially as their father only ever fitted seeing the children into own his plans – never in the best interests of the children. Diana described to us the awkwardness for them all at handover time.

We also gathered that many au pairs or mother's helps were also, in Clare's words 'a godsend – we would all gave gone under without Martina'. Clare felt that her mother's help provided some essential stability for her three boys and that while she was trying to negotiate events when her partner threatened to leave, her right hand was really there for the boys.

> 'There was one occasion just after he'd gone when Jan ended up putting us all to bed and bringing us hot chocolate: we all cried together. Jan gave me the opportunity to grieve and by the time I could no longer afford to keep her, I was steadier in myself. Jan got another job locally, so she could at times baby-sit and otherwise keep in touch with the family.'

Victoria

Both Victoria and Jan knew that although there had to be change it was very important for the children to see Jan – especially as contact with their father was sporadic.

> 'I said to the children's mother after the separation that we must not be too lenient on the children or they won't understand when we tighten up again on their behaviour. She said she knew I was right but was just trying to keep a peaceful atmosphere in the home.'

Bee

> 'When I was still married, I had an au pair and, during the week, the house ran like clockwork. At the weekend, when my husband was supposedly helping me with the children, there were tears and

137

*shouting. I began to wonder what kind of marriage I had if I valued the au pair so highly and the children were happier with Margot than their own father. Later, I realised this was the time when he was having an affair and resented being with the family. He then left us. Thank God Margot stayed on to help us deal with the trauma of it all.'*

Pippa

*'Inga, our au pair, asked me if she could be there for the return of the kids each Sunday night. I thought that was considerate of her to help the children, but years on I now think she was there for me. It was a dreadful time – a lot of shouting.'*

Lizzy

*'I had terrible trouble finding a reliable childminder for Alice and Tim. I had to change three times in the first year until I found someone I was happy with. Alice suffered a lot – as Tim was only a baby I don't really know if it affected him.'*

Sandy (mother of Alice, 3, and Tim)

# CONCLUSIONS

Grandparents, teachers and domestic help all can and do contribute to the welfare and support of families – especially those going through difficult times.

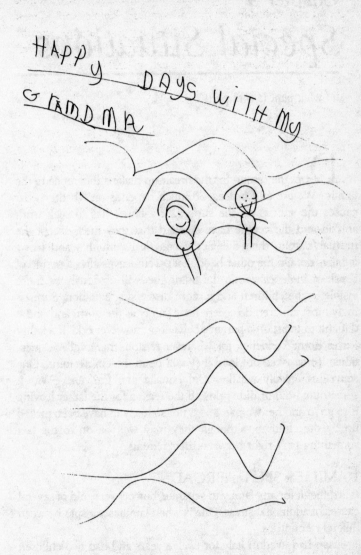

HAPPY DAYS WITH MY GRANDMA

# Chapter 9
# *Special Situations*

*'O what pain it is to part!'*

John Gay

DOES the reason for the break-up make a difference to the family? We are told it does. So much depends on whether what causes the split is on the surface. If a father has to seek work abroad and the couple have decided that they must accept the inevitable split, then the family can deal with this and many families do. On the other hand, if a parent leaves after a period of abuse or violence within the home this will obviously be more visible to the children and a more distressing situation. Surprisingly most children do accept their family as the norm and find it difficult to question a parent's behaviour, however odd. If a father leaves home suddenly, for whatever reason, there will be questions. If not asked out loud they will be in the child's mind. One source of anxiety will be, 'Did I make him go?' and, 'Was it something I did or didn't do?'. If the reason for the father leaving is to go to another woman this is not so likely to have been picked up by the children, although they may well be on to the fact something isn't right between their parents.

## FAMILIES SPLIT ABROAD

It is difficult for any family to separate, but we were told of several causes of additional stress. One is when families are split between different countries.

Susan had lived in Italy for twelve years and had two children aged 11 and 12 at the time of the break-up of her marriage. She told us she knew that her relationship wasn't perfect but described her surprise and shock when she returned to England (because her grandmother had a minor heart attack) and was told by her ex not to come back. She says she refused to accept her dismissal and she returned to Florence to sort out the problem. Six months later she was told to leave again. Sue says she just couldn't make it work by herself, but she had tried, not just for the children but because it had been a good relationship.

Alice said her situation had been similar – she had lived in Spain for nine years when her partner told her to go back to England with the children. Alice returned, penniless, with two daughters, 9 and 2. She says her family were supportive and her husband's parents urged their son to try again and not to leave it at that. She knows his parents miss their English grandchildren very much indeed – but offer little in the way of support.

Access arrangements were discussed between Susan and Alice.

*'I have always said he may see the children, or if he sends money and tickets I will take them to him, but other than empty promises he has made no attempt to see them and I cannot afford the trip. He has contributed nothing to their financial or emotional upkeep since the split.'*

Susan

*'At first he 'phoned regularly to talk to the children. The elder used to get upset and ask, "Why can't we go back to Daddy?" The younger one appeared not to react, except for recognition of his voice. The calls declined within two or three months and now appear to be settling at about six-monthly intervals. His family phone on birthdays and at Christmas and communications are good between us.'*

Alice

*'My elder child had to cope with not only losing Daddy but also learning English. She spoke Italian, and although she heard and understood English would never speak it while in Italy.'*

Susan

Alice said her two girls still occasionally ask why they can't go back to Daddy, but they alternate this with, 'I hate Daddy.' At the moment Alice is trying to help both daughters who talk anxiously about never having had a 'proper family'. Alice feels she has not got to the bottom of it, but she strongly suspects that something has triggered this off. She wondered if her daughters have been teased at school, or perhaps read something in the newspaper. Alice says she worries about the girls missing their dad and knows the importance of bonding between daughters and fathers is not exaggerated. Susan agrees, but feels any man can fulfil the role and occasionally her own father or a male friend fills the space.

Alice and Susan agreed that although financially they are far worse off than before, emotionally they have both created a stable home base for their family in England.

*'I feel the children are happier and better balanced with one parent who loves them and who tries to explain things honestly and without prejudice than in an atmosphere which varied from delight to despair.'*

Alice

*'I believe their father still loves them despite his seeming neglect. That is just part of his character; out of sight, out of mind and if there is a problem, ignore it, it will go away.'*

Susan

They did wonder, together, if their lot had been made more difficult for the children (no chance of access) or easier because they were not moving between two countries, let alone two parents.

*'Paolo was three when Stefano and I separated. I came home to my parents. I certainly had a small boy crying for his papa. Stefano and I both love Paolo and I think we both suffered seeing him suffer. We worked out a regime – I have Paolo during term-time and he goes to Rome for his holidays. We have agreed on one rule which is no tears at the airport – either from Mama, Papa or Paolo. Stefano and I both bend over backwards to help Paulo move from one culture to another but each time I meet him after a long holiday I am amazed at the sight of an Italian boy coming towards me. I love Italy and*

*Stefano loves England so we don't find it difficult to appreciate each other's values and way of life – so we reduce a pull in different directions for Paolo.'*

Esther

For these three women fear of abduction was not an issue. But from Eileen we hear a different story. Since the separation of Eileen and Mohammed, Aileen had been subjected to endless tugs of war and separations. Mohammed wants to return to the Middle East with his daughter, and Eileen feels forced to live in hiding with her (she is now 5). When contacting us, Eileen was desperate to ensure that we would give no identifying features. As Aileen has not seen her father for a year, Eileen had hoped she was forgetting the turbulent years when she had been pulled between them, but only this week Aileen had pointed to a man on a bus and said, 'Daddy?', and began to cry.

Reunite is a charity that will advise on what action can be taken and what the British government can do to help if a child is abducted. It comments:

*'Both parents in a dispute may believe they have the right to have the child living with them or to have contact with the child. Unless an amicable settlement can be reached, it is the courts of the country to which the child has been taken which will decide on these issues. Court orders of one country are not usually enforceable in another country.'*

# FATHERS IN PRISON

We spoke to probation officers and to organisations who befriend prisoners' wives, but there seemed to be no guidelines about what to tell the children, apart from an informal 'don't' or 'tell them he's working abroad'. Nevertheless, when a father goes to prison there will be questions – and therefore decisions to be made which may have long-term consequences (see Appendix II for useful addresses).

Kate explained how she dealt with the fact that her husband was sent to prison for a major offence, leaving her with a 2-year-old son. All the advice offered to her was 'don't tell the boy' but as she planned to visit her husband she thought this was bad, unrealistic advice.

*'I would have agreed, though, if it had been a short stretch, but 2-year-old boys grow up. So I told him the truth about his dad.'*
Kate

For Natalie the situation was different. She was already separated from her partner when he was arrested and sent to prison. Her son was 5 and she had no qualms about telling Tom that his father had gone to New Zealand. As Tom grew up he became increasingly curious about his father, and as a teenager talked of finding him. Natalie spoke to the probation officers at the prison which held Tom's dad and it was confirmed he would not be released for some time. Natalie was concerned about Tom, who was becoming restless and defiant: would it help him to know where his father was? Natalie knew that she wanted no contact at all with her ex-partner but she doubted whether she had the right to withhold information from her son. She found it impossible to get advice but eventually she decided to tell Tom the truth and to say he could write to his father in prison if he wanted to. Tom took the news very badly. Natalie understood that Tom had, in his mind, built up a romantic picture of his dad, and now he crashed down and became very depressed.

This happened in 1990 and in 1995 Tom is still depressed and has very low self-esteem. He has dropped out of school and Natalie has been unable to get any psychological help for him. At one time, she had been able to get an appointment for him with a psychiatrist specialising in adolescent problems but Tom refused to go to the hospital.

*'Tell the truth, or most of it, from the start. My partner and I separated years ago, but by God, his shadow has hung over us. Tom's dad is locked up for a violent crime – but Tom is paying a price too.'*
Natalie

*'Joe and I got divorced two years ago. He is now serving a very long prison sentence. This second loss has made explaining "Where's Daddy?" to our children very difficult to handle.'*

Mandy

When considering the plight of families where the father is in prison we were comforted to be told by a prison chaplain that in each prison there is always a chaplain to consult and to talk to.

'What shall we tell the children?' is a frequent question. Of course, each family is unique and what may feel 'right' for one, would be, perhaps, evasive and unthinkable for another. For some families, visiting father is a day out for the kids but for others dad has no contact with his family at all while in jail. Much, it appears, can depend on the type of crime and length of sentence, and on the distance of the prison from the home. Perhaps small children – we were advised – could be told, 'Daddy has to live somewhere else for a while' and as they grow older something approaching the truth should be attempted – keeping in mind, again, the type of offence and length of sentence.

The wife of one man in prison with a sentence of several years spoke to us of the hardship for the families. She knew of no other family in a similar position and believed her parents and brothers felt some shame. Even more than the financial worries, she was concerned about how this was affecting the children.

*'Life is bleak and we keep ourselves to ourselves. Sometimes I wonder who is in prison – him, or me and the kids.'*

Pam

*'My boys didn't have to ask "Where's Daddy?". They saw him leave the house with a detective on either side of him.'*

Eileen

*'I'd kill myself and Ricky rather than tell him where his father is.'*

Maureen

*'I'm not a religious person but it says in the Bible, "If one suffers, all*

*suffer" and when I look at my children missing their dad I know its true.'*

Annabel

A conservative estimate suggests over 100,000 children have a parent in prison in the UK. These children have committed no offence but feel the grief and loss caused by separation plus, often, discrimination and tremendous disruption to family life.

# MILITARY FAMILIES

For military families, there is perhaps always the feeling that 'Dad might be off to war', but the military environment can provide some support for the families and there is the feeling that 'we are all in it together – it goes with the job'.

Gillian, now a grandmother herself, can remember her father leaving the family to go to war. She can clearly remember the feel of his rough uniform and the brass buttons pressing into her as he hugged her goodbye and then she watched the soldiers marching off. She remembers feeling proud, like the other children, and she says she knew where Daddy and all the others had gone. The ceremony with which the men marched away was re-enacted in the playground for months.

*'I was too young to worry about whether he was coming back and we all marched around swinging our arms – we thought it was fun. Of course I didn't connect it then, but I started to be very scared that my mother would go away. I used to wake in the night and go and look for her, and I began to hate going to school. Even as a little girl I can remember being puzzled about that, because when I got to school I loved it but I just got tearful when I had to leave my mother and often faked a tummy ache. I don't know whether to laugh or cry when I tell you I couldn't eat peas!'*

Gillian

She went on to explain that as a 5-year-old looking at her lunch she became worried that if she put some peas on her fork she might leave on the plate the 'Mummy' pea and split the family.

Gillian remembers her eyes misty with tears and she can still see in her mind's eye the concerned looks on the faces of the grown-ups. She says she couldn't tell them what was wrong as she didn't know herself. Perhaps these signs of a child in distress are ones which we would now pick up more readily and help the child to find the words. Certainly, for Gillian and her friends, no one expected the children to be affected by their fathers' absences.

More recently, we heard of the Ryan family. Chris Ryan served in the SAS during the Gulf War, leaving behind a wife and daughter Sarah, aged 2. Five months after his return, Chris rejected his family.

The memory of death and survival consumed him, he became remote from his wife and child, and they returned to Ireland. What would Sarah have understood? Luckily Chris's wife Jan, with her own military background, had the understanding and sensitivity to help him to take time to recover from his experiences and they are reunited as a family now.

Lily (14) noticed the change in her father on his return from the Gulf War. 'Where **is** Daddy?' is also hard to answer when he is there physically, but not emotionally, for his daughter.

Combat Stress (see Appendix II for details) is an organisation which specialises in the care of men and women of all ranks discharged from the Armed Services who suffer from what was formerly called shell-shock. It says:

> 'War is hell, and hell is shell-shock. Combat Stress offers help and counselling to veterans from their early 20s to over 90 years of age – all who suffer from Post-Traumatic Stress Disorder.'

In the 1990s Post-Traumatic Stress Disorder, and the effect not only on the sufferer but on family life, is recognised and because of this there is hope that help can be found and marriages saved.

The cost to families cannot be calculated.

# CLERGY WIVES

The wife of a clergyman told us when a family such as hers breaks up, there are additional factors. Not only was there her own shock to deal with, but the shock of parishioners. Amy's losses included her husband and home, her status in the community, and her faith.

*'I felt so alone and although I had not brought about the break-up I felt that many of the people I had considered to be friends, looked at me with disappointment. It was as if I'd let them down. I suppose for people living around us we had, in a way, let them down. They lost their safety when they saw our family collapse. No one expects a clergy marriage to break down. But it happens. We were only a small community and my children had a hard time at school. I certainly felt at a loss about what to tell the children. I wish now I'd been more direct but I was so muddled myself I think I confused them even more.'*

Amy

*'The pressure of living on the job in the way we did was enormous. I felt under constant scrutiny – we had no private life.'*

Pamela

*'I had no one to talk to when I felt our marriage was failing. I felt disloyal if I even thought of talking about it to someone in the parish.'*

Betty

Broken Rites (see Appendix II for details) is an organisation which supports divorced and separated wives of clergy. It hopes that its work has helped, in a wider sense, to bring greater awareness and understanding of the causes of clergy marriage breakdown.

## DISABLED CHILDREN

The birth of a disabled child does put great pressure on a family. Many are able to bear this and to feel strengthened in doing so. However, for some families it is too heavy a burden and the marriage may crack under the strain of additional care for a child who is physically or mentally disabled.

Marie had two children and a good marriage, when a third – severely disabled – child was born.

*'Right from the start there were dreadful problems – Andy and Alison had been such good happy babies, but Amy cried a dreadful high-pitched scream nearly all the time. [Eventually a diagnosis of cerebral palsy was made.] If anything, things got worse as Amy grew older. Family outings became fraught and their father would take Andy and Alison off, leaving poor Amy and me behind. I realise now Jack couldn't come to terms with having a less than perfect child – so he cut her out of his life. He said I always put Amy first – I suppose I did, and I often resented Amy because of this. My mother looked after Amy one afternoon a week so that I could go into therapy because I felt so helpless most of the time. Jack did leave us and he left behind a split family. Andy and Alison's, "Where's Daddy?", had a very different, accusing ring to it whereas Amy's, "Where's Daddy?", was plaintive – she had never really known a daddy. "Why has he gone?" was truly heartbreaking to answer – Andy and Alison had their own idea of the answer and I spent a lot of time with them trying to explain it was not Amy's fault that we couldn't all be the family we once were. Therapy helped me to find the words to help the children.'*

Marie

Marie was right to be cautious about how she explained the position again and again to Amy. Barbara's experience in a similar situation was that her child, too, saw the father leaving as a direct result of her disability.

*'You see, Mummy, I know you and Daddy wanted to get married as you both look so happy in your wedding photos – then I was born and you were both unhappy and got divorced. I know you're unhappy now because you look sad and I see you crying.'*

Julie (Barbara's 11-year-old daughter)

Barbara told us she had not realised that the reason for a divorce which had taken place seven years before still weighed very heavily on Julie's mind. Barbara realised that what Julie said was partly true, that she did still look and was very sad. She had not been able to make a clean break in her mind with her ex-husband. To be so depressed so many years on was a strong pointer of many unresolved feelings. Barbara started to see a counsellor and she was taken aback by the fact there were so many conflicting feelings stored inside. Not only was Barbara carrying the grief of her broken marriage, but also she had not looked at her own feelings for caring on her own for a very disabled child. She realised that in order to move forward, a lot of the past had to be put into perspective. She was grateful for her daughter's insight.

## DEPRESSION

*'My husband became very clinically depressed. He became more and more silent and separate from us. The children could not understand why their once happy and loving father suddenly ignored them – and me. We did not realise what was happening.*

*The children were asking, "Where's Daddy?", and I certainly didn't know what to say. We just did not realise he was ill. Eventually, he did see a doctor and was admitted to a psychiatric hospital. I didn't know what to tell the kids. It is not only divorce that splits a family, mental illness can too, believe me.'*

Annie

*'My husband quite suddenly refused to get out of bed and go to work. He became suicidal and I needed a lot of help from my family. He wouldn't go to a doctor. Both of my daughters became very distressed and their schoolwork suffered. Although he still lived with us, in every other sense he had left us. He lost his job and after a serious suicide attempt left me too. I couldn't answer all the questions the girls asked.'*

Patti

*'I thought my husband was having an affair – he was so distracted. It turned out he was suffering from depression and he got treatment. Until he did, the whole family suffered and our marriage very nearly*

*broke up. Once he could accept help, I got help too from the hospital social worker.'*

Laura

## SEXUAL DIFFERENCES

*'When Andrew told me our marriage was over I truly could not believe what he was saying. As far as I had known in 14 years of marriage he had never looked at another women, and I said this to him.'*

Wendy

Six months after this, Wendy found it impossible to complete our questionnaire and asked to meet one of us. We understood it was not only pain but embarrassment which continued to make it difficult for her to confide the details. She said she still needed help to find the words to explain the events to herself, let alone to others. Andrew had fallen in love with his business partner. Andrew planned to move out immediately but Wendy managed to rally herself enough at that point to demand that he stay to tell the children himself. Andrew replied that he couldn't and left. Wendy, at her wit's end to know what to say to Hazel (8) and Carol (10), compromised by telling them that their father was away on business over half-term. She felt this would give her time to gather her thoughts and perhaps for Andrew to return. He did not, and Wendy knew she had to tell the girls more about what was happening. She decided to unfold the news in stages – the first was that Daddy did not want to live at home any more and was moving in with Charles. As the girls knew Charles quite well, they appeared to be not too upset about this arrangement and asked to see their father. It was arranged that Andrew would take them out to lunch, but what Wendy did not anticipate was that Andrew would take the girls back to his flat after lunch. The first thing Hazel said when she saw the one-bedroomed flat was, 'Where does Charles sleep?' Carol, too, was puzzled and made a joke of it by saying, 'Well you can't sleep together, you're not married!' Andrew met this by silence, but when he handed back the girls he told Wendy what had been said and asked her to put them in the picture. This she found impossible to do.

Since then, she has been greatly helped by her counsellor. Andrew has been seeing a therapist and together they have been able to discuss the situation with their daughters. They have both been able to find the words to do this.

*'I know my family and friends found it difficult to understand when I left home and moved in with Maureen. We had fallen in love. At first my husband didn't believe me, but eventually things settled down. I had taken my son Rory (who is 12) with me, and the trouble was he doesn't like Maureen and she doesn't like him. My ex has remarried and Mau and I are happy – Rory isn't, and I do feel bad about the fact that he does go quiet for long periods. But that's life. I don't know what my ex-husband has told Rory about my sexuality, but kids are tough, and I'm sure he will come to terms with knowing his mother is lesbian. I'm OK about it, so he should be too.'*

Louisa

It seems difficult for Louisa to believe Rory must have many unanswered questions and perhaps overwhelming feelings about the loss of his family.

## SEXUAL ABUSE

It is beyond the scope of this book to look in depth at the effects on families in which there is evidence of child sexual abuse, but the following accounts touch on some of the issues. Even an accusation which is proved to be unfounded leaves scars.

*'I've been having a terrible time. My son Peter had a son with Wendy who left him and had a second son by another man who disappeared. Wendy has now had a third son by a man she is living with and has said that Peter can no longer see his son or the other little boy, with whom he had formed a close relationship. Peter contested the lack of contact and so Wendy went to the police and accused Peter of sexually abusing the boys. Thank God the police thought she was lying but everything has been ghastly for everyone concerned and isn't over yet.'*

Nevil (a grandfather)

*'For me it all started the night the police came, arrested my husband and told me he was being charged with sexually abusing young boys.'*

Lisa

Lisa told us that in the following months more painful facts were revealed. Her husband had been abusing their elder son for three years, and their younger boy had seen it all. Lisa said she tried to talk to the boys about their pain and confused feelings about their dad and she explained to them, step-by-step, about the divorce. She decided they would stay in the same house, 'to give them security'. For herself, she sought counselling to work through her own pain. The Church was important to this family and Lisa reported that she and the boys felt a sense of belonging there. The boys have not seen their father since the day he left, at first because the Social Services wouldn't allow it, then because the court ordered that he only saw them with a chaperone. He never made any attempt to do that.

Lisa said she has devoted the last five years to the boys – they go youth hostelling, bird watching and swimming. She sees them growing more independent and confident each day. She says she has given her best to them, but is also looking to the future when she can take up more interests of her own. We feel Lisa's own sense of purpose and stability – backed by the Church which has always been important to her – has ensured that they all come through this as intact as possible. Lisa has had an eye on their external world and also their internal world, with the help of her counsellor.

Lisa and the boys look to the future with marked confidence and Lisa's own attitude to the trauma has greatly aided the boys recovery.

## FATHERS AND SONS/MOTHERS AND DAUGHTERS

We heard of teenage boys wanting to live with their fathers. Perhaps it feels 'macho' to leave Mum behind at a time when they would have been pulling away in any case. In our society it is still primarily the mother's task to take care of the very young, but in time the father becomes more important to the child. A boy needs to follow the example of a man in order to become a man himself and to help him break away from the strong, early bond with his mother. He will want to walk like dad, and talk like dad, to identify himself more and more with his father and to imitate him in many ways. It is often at this time that a boy's sexual curiosity is directed towards the intimate life of his parents and this can be confusing if the father is obviously involved sexually with another woman. A girl, on the other hand, is growing out of her complete dependence on her mother and begins to imitate her and at the same time direct her love towards her father. She can thereby enjoy a taste of mild flirting within the safety of her family. Again, it is distressing if the 'rival' in the little girl's eyes is seen to be, not her mother, but a woman who has 'stolen' her father away.

Ann told us that her little girl (6) had very strong feelings about her father's new girlfriend.

> *'Maggie makes my time at Daddy's horrible; she sounds so angry all the time. When I am with Maggie or think about her meanness it makes me want to cry. I hate feeling I have to be good all the time at Daddy's because if I'm not Maggie shouts at me or Sam and my tummy and throat hurt. I hate Maggie so much and I wish she and Janey [Maggie's new baby] were dead; sometimes I don't smile even a little bit the whole day at Daddy's because of Maggie.'*
>
> Ann's daughter (6)

The feelings children have towards the parent of the opposite sex are no less intense than the emotions of adults. At the time of the break-up of a family, the children go through a variety of emotions. On one level, they feel totally powerless about the changes around them; on another, deeper, level we believe a son at this stage in his development may have wanted his father to go, to leave his mother there for him. This is fantasy, but when this happens in reality and the father does go it is very difficult for a small boy to deal with.

*'One day I went shopping with my sister and my son Sam. Sam behaved disgracefully and we all arrived home exhausted and angry. My mother arrived and took Sam off for a private talk. With her he could cry and he said he didn't know what to do. Since Daddy had left he (Sam) had tried to help by carrying in shopping and things but when Mummy and Aunty Phil and he had gone shopping the two women had talked together all the time and told him to get out of the way while they loaded and unloaded the car.'*

Molly

A clear example of a small boy not knowing what or where his place is in the changing family. At the time of a break-up of a family, the children can feel very powerless, and they usually are.

It is all too easy to hold inside angry and frightened feelings, especially if the child is terrified the resident parent could leave home as well. Some children need help in being able to express their feelings and to be helped to understand that wishes do not automatically come true. When a child wants his or her parents to be together and cannot have this, it is a hard and painful lesson to learn – and it is made even harder if the child is feeling guilty for having angry thoughts and feelings towards their parents. It is only a small step for children to take, to believe that if they have these strong, murderous thoughts about a parent at times, then perhaps their parents feel like that towards the children! This is a very frightening thought indeed for a child to deal with and it is then that inner stress is shown, often by problems with behaviour or in bodily expressions. When Marie (in Chapter 2) told her daughter (2½) that Daddy wasn't going to live at home any more, Julie vomited and continued to do so. She continued for some years to show her anxiety and inner turbulence by a series of tummy aches and nausea.

*'I hate it when I go to Daddy's, I'm always disappointed because I think I'll have a nice time and I don't.'*

Liam (4)

# SAME MOTHER, DIFFERENT FATHER

Another possible cause of extra stress is where children share the same mother but have different fathers.

> 'My boy, Len is 12 and his sister, Karen, is 9. Now Len's dad does come around now and again – nothing regular – but when he comes he brings the boy a present. With Karen, it's a different matter. Her dad took off and I don't have any contact or support from him. The problems really show now they are getting older. Len grumbles enough because he doesn't see his dad often. He says he hates him, but when his dad arrives you should see how his face lights up. Karen can't understand why her dad isn't around. I've told her he is abroad, but that doesn't really help. So it's hard to answer your questionnaire because it's different for both children. I get upset when she hangs around Len and his dad, and Len gets furious. She's of an age now when she needs a father – I don't really know how to help her.'
>
> Gyll

Gyll's main concern is that she knows she feels guilty about Karen not having an available father and because of this tries double talk (as she calls it) to make her daughter feel better.

> 'I'll say something like "I told you your dad works abroad – and that's nice – now off to bed".'
>
> Gyll

She went on to say that in her heart, she thinks she is afraid to let Karen express her feelings about the situation. However, she worries that if she doesn't let Karen talk now, when she grows up will she have problems expressing how she feels about people? Gyll suspects that Len teases Karen and she is uncertain how to manage that. At present, she pretends not to hear the verbal digs her son gives to his sister.

Emily heard about Gyll's dilemma and told us she had been in a similar plight. Helen (9) and Pat (6) have different fathers. Emily said right from the start she had tried to get the girls to understand

156

that although they shared her and were a family, their background was not the same and in that way they were different, but both special. Emily's plan was to concentrate on the three of them being the family unit, and aunts and cousins were 'extra' family. If one of the girls' fathers was in touch – as occasionally they were – this was an extra bonus for one, but not a tragedy for the other. Emily said she did not feel guilty that neither of the girls had a father; life had just turned out that way, and perhaps that made it possible for her to have a more relaxed approach with the girls.

## PROBLEMS FOR THE ONLY CHILD

An only child can feel especially lonely at the time of the break-up of a family.

*'I longed to talk to somebody about what was happening, but instead I withdrew into my head and let my imagination keep me company. It helped blot out the noise of my parents screaming at each other.'*

Elspeth (19)

*'I still remember clearly Dad going – I wanted to run after him but at the same time stay and look after Mum. I think it did help my daughter to talk about her own very mixed and confused feelings when my husband left us. I told her I understood, and I do.'*

Ruby

If your own parents divorced, don't be afraid to tell your children about how you felt when it happened.

*'I was especially careful never to put Faith in the position of having to choose between myself or Frank.'*

Amelia (mother of Faith, 9)

Amelia talked about her concern that the divorce could burden their child and that as an only child Faith would have her loyalty to both parents severely tested. Amelia and Frank did see eye-to-eye on the need to reassure Faith that the divorce was not in any way her fault. Amelia kept watch on Faith's feelings, and not just her behaviour, but even with this care she reports that Faith showed a high level of anxiety.

*'I have one child, Peter (who is 13). He asked what the arrangements would be if we did split up. He said he would want to live six months with Dad and six months with me each year.'*

Susannah

*'My daughter was only 3 when we broke up. My ex would collect her most Sundays and although she would fuss a bit she mostly went off happily. That was OK for quite a while, but then he wanted her for the whole weekend. That's when the trouble started. By 5, she found she missed out on parties with school friends. When she came home she would be weepy and complain her toys were always in the wrong place. I thought we just had to go through this but it broke my heart when she said she missed my kisses on the weekends and her friends have a mummy and daddy all the time. I knew then that it had dawned on Mary that she was different from her friends, and that's when the questions really began to be asked.'*

Lucy

One complicated family situation equivalent to that of an only child developed for Angela and her children. When Bill left home, he left behind a wife and three children – two boys aged 14 and 13 and a little girl of 5 (Penny). Angela felt at times unable to manage as she was almost overwhelmed with fears about the future and grief over the loss of Bill. Contact was agreed but the boys found it increasingly difficult to return to their mother after a weekend away. Bill was a very sporty outdoor type and he and the boys would enjoy all kinds of activities. Where did this leave Penny?

*'Penny became more and more withdrawn and it started to be a regular thing that Bill would ring to make arrangements to collect the boys and as an afterthought, say, "Oh and do you think Penny will manage to keep up or should she stay with you this weekend?"'*

Angela

Angela was in a difficult position: if she urged Penny to go off with her brothers and father she knew Penny often felt out of things and, at times, a spoilsport; on the other hand, if she kept Penny at home with her she worried that in the future Penny might not understand how the family had become so divided. The boys went to live with their dad while Penny stayed with Angela. Although Angela did try to keep up some contact between Penny and her father, in practice it became difficult. Penny began to show signs of the deprivation: difficulty getting to sleep, bedwetting and becoming phobic about going to school.

A child therapist was consulted and worked with Penny and her mother to help them both see that Penny was terrified of losing her mother as she had lost her father and then her brothers. It wasn't that she was afraid of going to school, but rather that she was afraid that when she came home her mother would be gone too. Angela explained to us that she could understand why Penny was anxious and she herself was still concerned about the future effect on Penny, who had gone from being the youngest child in a boisterous athletic family, living in a large house, to an only child living in a small flat with a very un-sporty mother. The males had disappeared from both their lives and Angela says she had to struggle a lot to come to terms with this. It was hard to lose a husband; followed so closely by the loss of her sons. It became unbearable and Angela suffered from depression and serious weight loss. Nevertheless, she put her mind to helping Penny through this dreadful time.

The child therapist also suggested to Angela that she had some help for herself – after all Angela had lost two sons and a husband. Contact was seldom and Angela was bitter about the way Bill had left. Together with her counsellor, Angela looked at the grief and pain in her own life. Since the split, she had become very preoccupied with Penny's difficulties and had overlooked the psychological impact on herself. There had been massive changes in her life and as she began to feel calmer this, in turn, was felt by Penny. Angela said she pondered long and hard over this and enlisted the help of men in the family. With the support of her brother and brother-in-law and his children she made sure that Penny still received some of the rough and tumble she had been used to with her brothers. Angela tried to show Penny that an all-female home wasn't so bad and that girls could have a good time too.

This happened several years ago and Angela has remarried and now says she feels they have settled into a new family very happily. At 11, Penny has a new sister.

*'I do believe, though, that without therapy Penny may well have gone on believing that she had been left behind "just because she was a girl" and that wouldn't have helped her in later life I'm sure.'*
Angela

# OLDER WOMEN

Older women left by their husbands, often when their children are in their late teens or even young adults, need to be given a voice too. They would have had to find answers to difficult questions, even if they were couched in more sophisticated words than, 'Where's Daddy?'

Until the 1950s, marriage was a pension. So, what of the situation for those brides 30-odd years on? How did they manage? How has the women's revolution helped them? Already mothers in the swinging 60s, they were mostly untouched by women's liberation.

*'I was "there" all right in the 60s, but washing nappies – by hand – while singing along with the Beatles.'*

Jean (56)

*'When you got married in the 50s you got married and that was that. Or so I thought. We'd been married over 30 years when John told me he wanted a divorce before he was too old to start another life with someone else . . . much younger, of course. I was mortified and found it so painful to tell the children. My daughter pitied me and I thought that quite dreadful. My son asked me, "What have you done?" I cried for weeks. I didn't think he'd go, but he did.'*

Dorothy (68)

Dorothy went on to say that for her the most terrible part of the separation was the loneliness.

We heard a great deal about the embarrassment of telling older children that a marriage had failed. We also heard of the pain of women brought up and trained only to be wives and mothers who found they no longer had a job.

*'I was made redundant at 64 years old. I'd given my life to my husband. His work took us all over the world, so I had very few close friends. My children had been sent back to England to boarding schools so we weren't very close either. They didn't really want to know. I didn't know what to do with myself. Its no fun getting old, especially on your own.'*

Molly

*'I married when I was 19, and although I knew immediately after the wedding we were not suited we were together for 30 years before he decided to leave me. I had to get a job.'*

Ruth (54)

This was echoed time and again: 'I had to work', 'From part-time to full time', 'At 50 I had to look for a job', 'At my husband's insistence I had never worked, then at middle age I had to find employment'. 'My career has blossomed in a way that would not have happened if we had not divorced', and, 'I now have a full-time responsible job my husband would not have let me have if we had still been married.'

*'I was married in 1939 and had two little children when he left. I took a part-time job at 35/- per week and had to pay someone to give them tea and keep an eye on them. I had to pay half of what I earned.'*

Sonia

Sonia told us she did speak about her situation in front of the children to a close woman friend who needed to know all the details of Sonia's husband's behaviour because she had to appear in Court, to verify them. This was at a time when divorce procedure was more complex than it is today. Sonia considered the question of how the divorce affected the children.

*'I did not think so at the time as he was so moody and grumpy, but I realised later it did affect them. My daughter eventually became reunited with him, but my son refused. Years on he says he has missed a father figure.'*

Sonia

Sonia says she wished there had been counsellors around in her day. She says that her ex got all the blame because he left, but she added that he had a deep, and probably justified, grudge against her. She knows that she was:

*'Very repressed because of my upbringing and I did not care physically for him. Nowadays, I suppose I would have seen a sex therapist. I suppose many men would feel vicious with a wife who rejected them. On the other hand he knew I had been brought up with only an extremely strict and unfeeling mother, with no father.'*

Sonia

'My husband never even sent the children a birthday card after he remarried.' How tragic that such a feeling and thoughtful woman, who in the 1990s would have sought professional help, had to battle alone with her problem in the 1940s.

*'I was married at the end of the 50s, and life was so different then. I gave up the job I had in an office of course, and had a baby followed by another two years later. I certainly knew we were not a happy family but it never crossed my mind to do anything about it. A lot of my women friends weren't happy either but what was the alternative? Even in the 60s I didn't know anyone who was divorced. One just didn't!'*

Cynthia

Cynthia described a rather lonely life – her husband Arthur worked long hours in the City and Cynthia busied herself with bringing up the children. The fact that Arthur had very little to do with the actual day-to-day task of childcare was accepted as the norm. When the children were in their early teens Arthur dropped his bombshell – he was involved with someone else. He told them that on leaving he would support the children and Cynthia financially until the children finished their education. He told Cynthia that she did not need legal advice and if she did not accept his offer, she would get nothing (when Cynthia no longer had to care for the children, her husband stopped her maintenance). In a way, Cynthia says, life went on – the children had had very little close contact with their father and it wasn't for some years that Cynthia realised that they had been more affected by the break-up than she had thought. For five years Cynthia was preoccupied with keeping up appearances and she told us it is only by looking at their lives now that she can see the impact the separation and loss of their father had on the children.

*'My daughter has only had one man in her life, and she was terrified he would abandon her. My son is gay and has been in therapy, during which he became aware of the enormous loss of his father. I suppose I should have prepared myself for that moment [when she had to seek employment] – nowadays women would. I'd only worked as a typist before I was married, and I liked being a housewife and caring for a family and garden. My children begged my husband to go on giving me an allowance, but he was adamant and by then he did have another family to support. My mistake was not getting proper legal advice when he left, but I was afraid to make much of a fuss.'*

Cynthia

This theme, of not making a fuss, was repeated. Molly was left by her husband after 35 years of marriage. She finds it in her heart to be forgiving, and she certainly takes part of the blame for the failure of a lengthy relationship.

*'We expressed our love by parenting our children – I thought that
was enough: it wasn't. I found that out too late. Once the children
left, we had nothing. I'm pleased for him that he has found some
happiness with a new partner.'*

Molly

Molly did add, though, that the thought of the future alone
frightens her. Her children are somewhat distanced from her since
the separation, and she finds it very hard to come to terms with
their air of disapproval and disappointment.

*'I always knew my husband had girlfriends and as long as he was
discreet and kept it from the children I turned a blind eye. The
shock came when Richard had his 70th birthday and told me he
was leaving me to live on his own. I doubted that, and I was right –
he was leaving to live with a woman I've known about for years. He
told me that he would continue to come to me for Sunday lunch,
and the children need not know. The children! They are parents
themselves! Of course I told my daughters, and really they don't
want to know – if anything, they are unsympathetic and get
embarrassed when I try to tell them about their father and his
women. I say, "Your father's with his whore" and they don't like
that.'*

Marjorie

Marjorie implored us to pass on the lesson from her experience
to other women. The message, bluntly, is not to wait or turn a
blind eye.

*'I did, and I got no thanks for it. I suppose over the years I baulked
at what to tell the children (and myself) and let him get away with
murder. I've been the loser all round.'*

Marjorie

What also hurt Marjorie was the attitude of her children, who let
her know they thought she had been a fool and would be turning
herself into her husband's mistress if she let him come home on

Sundays. Sadly, Marjorie felt neither her children nor her grand-children understood how ashamed she was of the way her life had turned out. Her bitterness and sharp tongue was a cover for this. She continues to welcome Richard for lunch each Sunday. The children and grandchildren no longer share the family meal. Elinor, their eldest daughter, says she cannot stand her mother's pain and has put an embargo on her mother phoning to talk about what Dad is up to now. It seemed to us that the family had been kept together by everyone turning a blind eye, but once the truth was out it became too awful to discuss. Elinor said she wouldn't dream of discussing her father's private life, and so keeps up the illusion he is living by himself. Marjorie goes on hoping that by being accommodating Richard will come home to stay.

> *'I discovered my husband was having an affair and that she was pregnant. Despite my shock, hurt and terrible anger, I was convinced I would not let my husband leave. It helped me that she lost the baby, but I did everything I could, above board and below, to save my family the pain of splitting up. Twenty years on, we are still together but I realise now that we have many unsolved problems between us and a whole area of life not acknowledged to each other. And did we do the right thing? Two out of our three children are now divorced (both with small children themselves) and one has never had a serious relation-ship. I know I am not happy and have suffered greatly with my chosen life of denial.'*

Joan

> *'I was 55 when my husband left me. I have managed to work and keep busy but I do not believe I will ever have another relationship. I've forgotten how to talk to the opposite sex.'*

Delia

> *'My husband divorced me and said he couldn't take the respon-sibility of marriage and parenthood: I had a 6-month-old baby. He went on to marry (and divorce) seven more times.'*

Laura

*'I am so lonely. A woman who sets out to be a single parent from the start is able to cope with the problems of prejudice, suspicion of "friends" and all the other experiences which the once-married single parent is usually unable to cope with. She never set out in the first place to be a single parent. I have just joined Dignity and I have even been away for the weekend with some members. I'm making new friends and we are all struggling to come to terms with the loss of a partner through divorce.'*

Annie (40)

*'When he left me the children were teenagers. I had no choice but to put the children first and I have denied the chance of my own identity. But what else could I have done? The children had no-one else and at least I have the satisfaction that they have grown up into responsible human beings. It is my fault they now see me as a colourless doormat.'*

Joan

All these women speak of the difficulties of being propelled by external events into a very different life from the one they had expected to live. Whereas the younger women spoke of shock, disbelief and grief, these women spoke more of humiliation, shame, disappointment and bereavement.

*'I didn't even have the dignity of being a widow – I was just an old woman whose husband didn't want her any more.'*

Pat

# HALF AND STEP BROTHERS AND SISTERS

The difficulties some children have in accepting step or half brothers and sisters could take up a whole book. We cannot address them fully here, but we will touch on some of the common experiences.

Jonathan (6) was always very articulate when describing feelings for his new half brother.

*'I wish I was able to hold Robert, then I would be able to throw him*

166

*out of the window. It makes me angry and so sad when he calls my
daddy "DaDa"; he was my daddy first and I wish he and Sue were
dead!'*

Jonathan

It must be so hard for a little boy of 6 to understand why his
father has left his family. Even if you manage to get him to
understand it was a 'Daddy doesn't love Mummy any more but
will always love you' situation, how can he understand the fact that
his father has left him and Mummy and now has a new son who he
does live with?

*'As an adult and mother I find it hard sometimes to understand it,
let alone if I was 6 years old.'*

Lucy

*'I was shattered when my husband left us and then had a baby with
his new woman. The girls used to spend every other weekend with
their father and his new family. To me, they would always pull faces
about the baby. One day I went to my youngest daughter's school
and read in her news book, "Today I went to my brother's birthday
party", together with a drawing of a tea party. I asked her about
this, and she looked uncomfortable so I said to her, "Little David is
not part of my life, but he is of yours and its quite all right for you to
say you like him." I hoped by saying the words aloud to her I would
help her to feel freer about the mixed feelings she has inside her.'*

Lindsay (mother of two daughters, 9 and 7)

# When the woman leaves

Women leave their families too and those who spoke to us said
they had to cope with enormous disapproval from almost everyone they knew.

*'I left Tim. I'm not proud of it, but I had had enough and left with
the children. We went to live with Brian and for the first time in
years I felt at peace. The children did ask about their father and
whether he still loved them, and I found that very painful. He did, of*

*course, but I wanted them to learn to love Brian. I didn't really answer them; I feel really bad about that now. I don't think they have ever forgiven me for that.'*

Melanie

*'I had an affair and left the children with my husband. After a few weeks I realised I had made a terrible mistake, but Joe wouldn't take me back. He said I was "soiled goods". Tim's wife started divorce proceedings too – so two families got smashed up. The children miss me and want me home. I've split my family and the pain is unbearable. The only way to escape the pain inside seemed to be to take my own life. I took all the sleeping pills my doctor gave me. I was discharged from hospital last month. I still think about suicide but I can't do it – I think of the children. Tim and I both wish we could turn the clock back. We both urge anyone tempted to start an affair simply do not do it. The price is very high. For us, the price was too high – we've both lost everything.'*

Elizabeth

*'The reason for the break-up of our marriage was very private. It was sex. Bob wanted sex all the time and after six years I couldn't deal with it any longer. He wasn't open to reason or discussion. He wanted to have sex, I won't call it making love, often three times a night, and that was every single night. I couldn't tell friends or family, I was too embarrassed. The rest of our life was pretty good: we had two beautiful children, a lovely house, an active social life and I loved that part of my life. No-one could understand why I left – taking the girls with me – and I went through agonies trying to find answers to their questions. Bob was frantic to have us back, the girls wanted their father and both families thought I had gone mad. I tried telling my doctor, but he made a joke of it. I told Bob he should get treatment, but he couldn't see why. I couldn't tell and Bob wouldn't, so most people are still mystified as to why we split up. It would be wrong of me to tell the girls, even when they are grown up, the reason for our eventual divorce. I concentrated on trying to reassure them that their dad loved them and I let him see*

them whenever he wanted to. He is going to marry again soon, and I do wonder how that will affect the girls.'

Beryl

'I left my three daughters – I had to get away. Four years on I realise I was depressed then and should have got help instead of leaving. I hardly have any contact. They were told I'd gone because I didn't love them and I can never mend the scars we all have.'

Angela

'I dread to think what my husband would have told the children if I had gone instead of his leaving us.'

Lisa

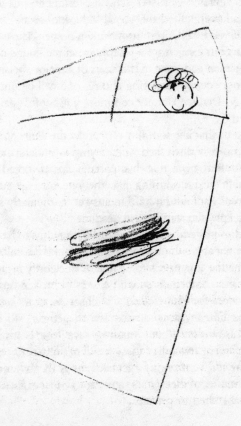

# Chapter 10
# *The Media*

*'Lord what fools these mortals be!'*

SHAKESPEARE

## THE INFLUENCE OF THE PRESS

'Divorce damages your children', shouted the headline in the *Daily Mail* (22 September 1994). The Government's Chief Medical Officer had highlighted the social, educational and health problems suffered by children from broken homes. The evidence for his conclusions came from a Joseph Rowntree Foundation survey and Dr Calman had gone to the heart of a major social issue. The fabric of our society is altering and no-one will be untouched by this change. Divorce is more common, but not less painful for all concerned.

Pat told us that her son, Jim (10), read the *Daily Mail* headline and became very distressed when trying to understand how that applied to him now that his parents are divorced. Was the Government health warning like the one on cigarette packets, he enquired? Pat found it hard to answer, particularly as she was, herself, deeply shocked by the headline.

Rose, who was married to a celebrity, urged us to be very blunt and forthright about the amount of pain around the collapse of any family, whether it happens to be that of a celebrity or not. She felt that the media bombards us with details of broken relationships: 'Another No.1 for Phil Collins', 'Michael Aspel makes whoopee with Irene Clark', 'Sting dumps stylish actress', 'Richard Gere trades in his model'. What is missing, says Rose, is any hint of the heartache and distress all of these headlines must conceal. Indeed, perhaps we really do begin to get taken in by the rather daring and dashing attitude of these stars, and rapidly lose sight of the tears that must be shed in private.

*'In your book, please do emphasize the pain. When Rob left me I felt I'd been skinned alive. He may have been making whoopee but he was cruelly abandoning me and our 10-year-old. It is no fun being dumped, believe me.'*

Rose

*'It was difficult enough dealing with the shock of a divorce, but then I had to take on board all kinds of things, like we were now a "one-parent family", and that my children were growing up in a "broken home": the very words made me shiver. Greg and Peter were constantly asking me questions about issues around single parents. Mostly they stemmed from things they had seen on TV or read in the papers. The newspaper articles affected them more than what other kids said because, "newspapers don't lie do they, Mum?".'*

June (mother of Greg, 12, and Peter, 14)

It is difficult to pick up a magazine or newspaper that does not dwell on the dark side of divorce and the possible harmful effects on the children. It is important to remember that children read the papers too, and their questions must be addressed even if only to provide them with some answers for when peers ask them questions.

The media gave an unreasonable amount of space to the very public way in which the Prince and Princess of Wales separated. Speculation about the children became fair game for many journalists. Like all children of high-profile marriages, William and Harry must surely have had a great deal to absorb and to deal with in private.

Reading about parents in the newspaper – whether royal or not – can be a very dreadful experience, especially for an adolescent, when there is disclosure of an extra-marital sexual relationship. It is right that children – particularly in their teenage years – should be kept factually informed, but it is not in anyone's interest for them to be told details of their parents' private lives. Unfortunately this does happen in cases widely reported by the press, especially when there is a sexual angle to the story.

*The Times* (27 March 1995) had an article quoting the Joseph Rowntree Foundation, openly acknowledging what a few years ago would have been unsayable: 'Children who experience divorce and family conflict are more likely to suffer educationally and psychologically than those whose parents stay relatively happily together.'

> *'I know my two will read* The Times *today and ask me "Mum, is this true?" It's at times like this I really hate Patrick for what his fling has done to our family. I hope she was worth it.'*
>
> Margaret (mother of two children, 14 and 16)

Grace read a report in the press from a professor of child and adolescent psychiatry about depression in children who 'lack adult support'. She found this such gloomy reading that she spoke to close friends about the fact that depression in childhood interfered with school work and the forming of relationships. Grace was particularly concerned because after the recent break-up of her family, her ex-husband moved abroad to work and her son Jack (12) had begun to fail badly at his schoolwork and also was becoming isolated. She found out more about the work of Professor Goodyer, who published a paper (*Journal of the Royal Society of Medicine*, June 1994) on the impact of recent life events in anxious and depressed school-age children, and this in turn was taken up by the media. His findings suggested that 'multiple exit events' (as he calls major separations) may not exert their effects until late in the child's life. Two or more losses are significantly more likely to be reported in the past history of anxious or depressed children.

Grace was somewhat comforted at first: as far as she could tell Jack had no other undesirable experiences of loss in his life. She, herself, was in therapy and her own mental health was being monitored. Grace was concerned to read that one adversity may facilitate the onset of another and for this reason she enlisted the help of teachers and friends to try to minimalise Jack's loneliness. He had been an outward-looking boy and the loss of his father and his subsequent loss of pride in his work and lack of friends alerted

Grace to possible future difficulties. She felt able to circumvent these events by being aware and by understanding more about Jack.

Although, as in Grace's case, articles in the press can fire the reader to find out more than is reported, and then to use the information in a thoughtful way, some women sink under the endless gloomy prognostications about children from one-parent families.

A report of two runaways trying to reunite their parents attracted the attention of parents and children alike (*The Times*, 30 January 1995). They left a note for their parents: 'get in touch with Mam – when she comes back we will come back.'

> *'I comb the papers for comments on single-parent families and the kind of "Divorce hits families harder than death" headlines. I always make sure I talk to the children about these articles. Sometimes they make us laugh. Did you know that you can get divorce greetings cards now? I saw one which says, "All Purpose General Divorce Card" and inside, "Good riddance". We have fun making up things we could say on a card to my ex – if I knew where he was, that is.'*

> Beryl

The media does, of course, also cover divorce in a more serious way. The work of Dr Martin Richard, director of the Centre for Family Research at Cambridge University, has attracted attention. His survey into the effects of divorce on children (based on children born in one week in March 1958 and followed to their present ages of 37) convinced him that low self-esteem and poverty after divorce is the reason why so many children from broken homes find their schooling is affected. A great deal of media space was also given to the Chancellor's recent proposal of changes in legislation.

The banner headlines about family strife are, however, often more eye-catching than serious research and comments on the changes in our society.

# THE CINEMA AND DIVORCE

Family strife is a popular topic for films.

In 1927, a Gary Cooper film *Children of Divorce* focused on what was then a relatively rare situation. The young women in the film are obviously from a wealthy family, presumably because at that time only the rich could have afforded a divorce or have weathered the subsequent scandal.

Film makers since that time have used the drama of divorce in many ways. Three films that spring to mind are: *Kramer v Kramer*, *Mrs Doubtfire* and *Damage*.

The film *Kramer v Kramer* showed how even a 'nice and sympathetic' father and mother can allow a situation to deteriorate into a battle which can only harm their child. *Mrs Doubtfire* offered a more hilarious version of a broken family, but did not really disguise the heartache of all the family members involved. The writer of *Mrs Doubtfire*, Anne Fine, a well known children's author, also wrote *Step by Wicked Step*, in which a group of children is taken on a holiday. What emerges is that what the children have in common is the fact they all have two emergency telephone numbers, two homes, two families: they are all children from broken homes (see Appendix II for other books on divorce for children).

We are, perhaps, left stunned after seeing Louis Malle's film *Damage*, in which the hero (Jeremy Irons) falls in love with his son's girlfriend, Anna, and becomes sexually involved with her. This, of course, eventually destroys the whole family but the Minister of State, played by Irons says, 'It will be hard for Martin (his son) but he's young, he'll get over it.' This misconception is one for us all to keep in mind. How comfortable it must have been to believe that children of any age did not notice what was going on in their parents' life and, if they did, were very resilient.

# BOOKS AND DIVORCE

It is important to search out books to read to the children. Jean told us what happened when she read *Dinosaurs Divorce* to her son, Ben (7).

*'It was the first time since his dad left that he became outwardly
interested in what was happening to them and would ask what
divorce meant.'*

Jean

Jean felt it gave her (and Ben) a forum in which to talk about the
things that needed to be said. He understood that Mummy and
Daddy were getting 'unmarried' but he might hear other people
talking about divorce and now he would know what that word
meant.

Relate has a series of books covering most aspects of separation
and remarriage (see Appendix II).

# DIVORCE ON TV

Joan Bakewell (BBC1 *Heart of the Matter*, 5 February 1995)
discussed the problem surrounding contact. She interviewed
women who wanted, above all, to get their children's father out
of their lives. One woman said poignantly, 'He never looked after
them once when we did live together; why should he see them
now?' The debate raged over whether, if the case went to court, the
mother should be sent to prison for obstructing her children's
rights to know their father. Mothers have been sent to prison for
defying the court and for not agreeing to contact. In most cases this
has been where there has been excessive drinking or violence but a
child watching such a programme might be filled with fear that such
a thing could happen to his or her family.

June told us that she often has what she calls a general discussion with her children (12 and 14); she said she doesn't make
things too specific to their situation, but picks up something from
a soap and gives the children a chance to talk about different
relationships they see. She hopes this gives them room to air
anything that puzzles them.

The Children Act states clearly that the interest of the child must
come first – but for many women wishing they could start a fresh
life it is hard to hold on to the thought that for most children no
contact equals bereavement.

After the *Heart of the Matter* programme, Nellie told us that her son (then 14) became morose and difficult. Nellie associated his change of mood with the programme and asked Hugh about it. He replied with a torrent of abuse and accusations. Hugh's bottled-up fury about not knowing his father poured out as he told his mother she had ruined his life by getting rid of his dad and not letting Hugh have contact with him.

*'Everyone knows that kids like me with no dad, have problems.'*
Hugh (14)

This exact conversation was echoed in the soap *Eastenders* (February 1995) and it is likely that Hugh's feelings would be experienced by countless other children. Nellie says that she was not sure whether or not to excuse herself and therefore damn Hugh's father, or to protect her ex and take the flak herself. What she did was to hear Hugh out and to say that perhaps it was time that she told him more of the facts about his dad. Nellie said she had hoped that as her ex had disappeared out of her life (his choice), she had believed he had disappeared out of Hugh's mind. She added that Hugh hadn't seen his dad or heard from him since he was one. Nellie described to us how she would have liked to tell Hugh how his dad had really been, but instead she searched her mind to give Hugh some 'facts' about his dad. She told him his father had blue eyes – like Hugh – and that he played football – like Hugh – and that he was very tall. Hugh asked why they weren't together as a family and Nellie frantically tried to think of an answer and said that she would tell him about that another day. She then talked over the problem with her sister and friends and after some rehearsal was able to tell Hugh a straightforward, but not emotionally overloaded, view of what happened 13 years before.

*'On reflection, Joan Bakewell did me a favour. She didn't put ideas of contact into Hugh's head; it was clear they had been there for years. The programme provided an opportunity for us to have a long overdue discussion.'*

Hugh's mother

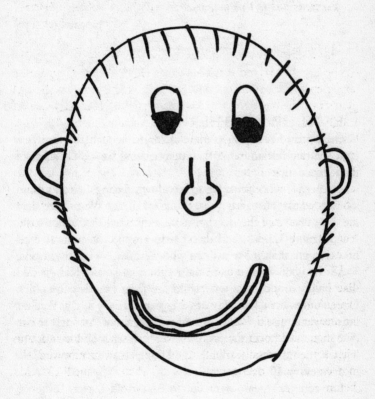

# Chapter 11
# *Death in the Family*

*'If you wish to draw tears from me,*
*you must first feel pain yourself.'*

HORACE

*'Any man's death diminishes me.'*

JOHN DONNE

## DEATH OF A FATHER

Mothers may have to help their children through the loss of a father through death rather than divorce, and we look at some of their experiences here.

Are people more sensitive to a widow's feelings than to those women whose husbands walked out on them? We believe they are. The results of the questionnaire confirmed that widows did receive more support and direct help around the time of their bereavement than those women who were left for other reasons.

All the widows who were the mothers of small children said they had plenty of help with childcare from friends and family. One young widow, Isabella, with a 1-year-old baby told us that her little boy did miss his father but reacted even more strongly to her own signals of hopelessness. Isabella's mother took little Paul to live with her for about 6 months, and Isabella saw him for a couple of days every 10 days or so.

The country's heart went out to 8-year-old Lucien Laurence after his father had been murdered. Lucien wrote to Father Christmas: 'I need my daddy back to help me to stop my mummy and sisters from crying.'

We know of so many children who carry the same terrible burden of grief, but cannot express it so clearly or openly. Lucien's words go to the heart of the matter and therefore touch us all.

No-one would expect him to be 'OK' or 'not really noticing', comments we hear from some adults about a father's sudden absence, but under different circumstances.

## Telling the children

Isabella's husband (who was 30) walked out of the door and never came back; he died playing squash. Isabella says she had no choice but to tell the children in one fell swoop and she told them in bed the morning after he died. Her middle boy, Gary (3), went 'really manic' for a while and then 'slightly over active'. He was desperate all the time to see his father. The 5-year-old, Clive, was very open and direct with his questions: 'How did his heart stop?', 'Why did he die?' and, rather frantically, 'If he died then can you?' Isabella could understand that his main concern was that she or anyone he loved might die immediately too.

Her 5-year-old was the most affected and continued to be very worried about deaths of other people. In reply to the barrage of questions, especially from Clive, Isabella says she told them as many facts as she could without worrying them, and tried to make it perfectly clear time and again that their father was dead, in heaven, and that they would never see him again. Two years on, Isabella reports the children are well and she considers herself content with the way they have all come through this terrible time.

Claudia says that although she felt overwhelmed by grief when her husband died, her daughter (Patti, 4) did not show signs of missing him or even much curiosity about what was happening and where he was. Patti was simply told he had 'passed away'. After all, said Claudia, he worked six days a week and on Sundays played golf so he hardly impinged on a little girl's life. Perhaps Claudia should have raised and then answered some questions which must have been somewhere in Patti's mind, but Claudia was adamant that this was not so and may have served to 'put ideas into Patti's head'.

We heard that Claudia was supported in her view by her own family and friends: 'Patti is too young to notice', 'She'll soon forget him', 'Don't say anything, don't upset her, she's only little', although one aunt did warn Claudia that her own withdrawal into mourning could seem like another loss for Patti. A child's concept of death can be hidden in the magical thinking of early childhood and it is possible that by simply being told her father had 'passed away', Patti could think of death as a pleasant trip to a far away country. However, we believe Patti would have fantasies about her father's disappearance which might be unspoken or not even consciously available to her at this time, even to the extent of wondering if she herself had caused her father to vanish to this other place. Only time will tell, but we do believe that Patti must have been aware of the changes around her and we do wonder about her apparent lack of curiosity. Even a father working six days a week does impose the presence of a man about the home.

Nine months later as Claudia started to emerge from her own shattering grief she began to see signs that Patti did have some anxieties, but Claudia still maintains that these were brought about by the rapid changes in childcare after the bereavement when she was unable to care for her daughter herself. Claudia does not believe Patti has been affected by the death of her father.

Rosemary was only in her mid-20s when her husband died suddenly after a short illness. She told us that all the questions we listed that children ask did apply in her case but seemed to be imposed in a much more subtle and unconscious way. It seemed to her that children (hers were 6 and 3 at the time of their father's death) do understand about death and that it is final. Rosemary thought that losing a father by death rather than by separation or divorce must be very different and that this is conveyed in many ways to children. Rosemary told them, on her own and immediately, that their father had died. She says she just kept solely to that fact at the time, and that other information was given in stages. Inevitably, she reported, she did talk about her situation to other people within the children's hearing.

Robbie (5) was found in the churchyard looking for his father's grave. He asked, 'Where is Daddy?' and went on to say that 'Everyone knows heaven is not in the sky.' He had not been told by Rosemary that his father had gone to heaven.

Agnes (3¼) asked why, if Daddy had died and gone away for good, had he not taken his briefcase? Both children, Rosemary said, asked why she had killed Daddy. Rosemary's children are now 19 and 17; she has no doubt that losing a father in early childhood affects children badly in adolescence and problems are then much more difficult to relate back to their early loss. She says that that is when outside therapeutic help is needed.

*'How to help – a lot of talking and just common sense I'd say.'*
Agnes

Later, she said her main concern over her life with her three children was the total lack of energy she had. Agnes told us that loads of her friends rang or called round to offer support whether they understood or not, but she wasn't that interested in socialising. It was all she could do to get the children to school, pick them up and get them to bed, so she could collapse herself. Her husband had died only seven months ago.

Ellie's children were adolescents when their father died after a year-long illness and, she says, they were involved all through. Ellie and the children were with Brian when he died. Her eldest child, Barry, was at home when his father became ill and it was he who, before Ellie could stop him, raced out to tell his sister that their father was desperately ill in hospital with a brain tumour. Barry was a medical student so he found out for himself what the prognosis was likely to be. Ellie feels Barry suffered a great deal as a result of his father's death and was left struggling with his studies. Ellie says that because she was aware of the stress on Barry she tried to protect him from looking after her and, in retrospect, feels she erred on the other side so that he felt excluded from her practical and emotional support. It became very difficult for them to talk. Ellie did receive help from the hospice social worker, and went back to see an analyst she had worked with years before. He died too, and Ellie suffered another bereavement. Ellie and her daughter had endless discussions about why it happened and she felt they were trying so hard to watch out for each other that it was difficult to find private space to feel their own grief. After some months the three of them met with a therapist as a family to get them communicating again and try to understand how each was coping with the loss, not only of Brian as a husband and father, but the loss of the family as they had known it.

## Children remember

We also heard from women who remember their father dying when they were children and they were able to tell us more about the way they saw the events at this time.

> *'I was four when my father died. I can remember very clearly that there were suddenly lots of people in the house and Mum was crying. I can also remember my nan saying to me I had to be a big girl now and help Mum. I just didn't make any connection that it had anything to do with Dad not being there. For a long time my mum used to sleep a lot and I know I sat quietly outside her room – I didn't play because I didn't want to wake her. I don't know if anyone did tell me Dad had died.'*
>
> Colette (26)

> *'I knew Daddy was ill. I was taken to see him in hospital. I was 8 at the time, and just thought he'd get better. One morning my Granny told me he wasn't coming home, but had gone to sleep. It didn't make sense to me but I could see from the grown-up's faces that I shouldn't ask questions. A few days later, I think it was, I asked if we could go to the hospital to visit, and my grandad was so angry with me I started to cry. Looking back, I suppose they all found it difficult to tell me. I had, and still do have, trouble getting to sleep.'*
>
> Susan (24)

Yet again, we encounter children who do not think they were told what was happening, but from adults we hear of lengthy discussions of how to tell children about separation around divorce and death. Perhaps the adults did think they told the children but it was not in a way the child could understand.

> *'When I was told Pa had died I asked if he'd gone to heaven and was told he had. That worried me, because I knew the next-door*

*neighbour's dog had died and gone to heaven and Pa hated that dog. I was 9 years old.'*

Kitty (30)

*'Dad died when I was about 6. I don't remember much of what I was or wasn't told. I only remember that suddenly everything seemed upside-down. My gran came to stay and I was always being sent out of the room to play. I was pretty sad but I don't think I knew why. I thought everyone was cross all the time and I didn't like that. I found it difficult to get to sleep – I used to sit on the stairs and try to hear what the grown-ups were saying. I still find it hard to get to sleep. I wonder if I always will?'*

Jackie (21)

*'My father died when I was nearly four – I don't know what I was told. I do know that, when I was about seven, I used to go into the churchyard on my way home from school to see if I could find his grave. I used to pick flowers and put them on one of the graves. I couldn't find my dad's. I did that for years. I didn't tell anyone.'*

Hazel (32)

# SUICIDE OF A FATHER

Suicide is perhaps one of the cruellest ways to lose a member of the family. So many questions are left unanswered and so many people are scarred by the event.

*'Three years ago my husband killed himself. We never got to the bottom of why he did it, and none of us had any idea that anything was wrong. Even now, I don't think people can believe that, but neither I nor our families thought that there were problems. Our children were then aged 6, 8 and 10; we were an ordinary family. It was as if a bomb went off and we still haven't recovered from the blast. When I was told by the police, I could only think there had been a dreadful mistake, in fact when Bob kept asking, "Where's Daddy?" I turned to him and said not to worry, Dad would soon be home to sort all this out.*

*I thought I was going mad with grief, whilst trying to find a way to hold the family together. Bob – only 8 years old – was quite frantic to know what had happened. I had no answers.'*

Celia

Friends and family urged Celia not to tell 6-year-old Amelia anything of what had happened but Celia's instinct was to tell her as much – or as little – as she knew.

*'After all, we four had to stick it out together. I couldn't stop the children hearing what was being discussed – almost without exception anyone offering condolences also said why do you think he did it?'*

Celia

She felt that if her husband had had a heart attack or been hit by a bus, some sense could have been made of his death and that, for a while, she even doubted all her memories of happy family occasions.

Suicide leaves a pall over life before the event. Celia and her children searched for an answer and she commented that it wasn't only the children who asked continually, 'Was it something I did (or didn't) do?' Even after a year, Celia felt she and the children were in deep and troubled mourning.

*'Don't tell me children don't feel grief or can't mourn; all my three were shattered.'*

Celia

We believe it is only because children have difficulty finding the words to express their feelings that so many adults are able to overlook children's pain of bereavement.

Celia searched her memory and recalled that her most usual reply to all her children's questions was, 'I don't know.' Three years on, she wishes she had been able to be calm and wise when talking to her children at the time of their father's death. William (now 13) has been badly affected and he has some difficulty concentrating for long periods. On the advice of a friend, Celia and the children are about to see a family therapist.

*'My husband killed himself when I was pregnant with my daughter. I don't know why – I thought we were happy. Four years on, I have remarried and my life is back together again. Not for my daughter though and the questions about her daddy are just beginning to come.'*

Liza

In 1980 the rock star Ian Curtis hanged himself when his daughter was 1. His wife Deborah has just published her story. Deborah says Natalie (now 16) asks about her dad all the time, and sometimes it's been difficult but, 'From now on I'll be able to hand the book to her . . . it's all in there.' Yet another way of coping with so many questions and so few answers.

## DEATH OF BOTH PARENTS
We were deeply shocked by the reply from one woman, now in her 50s, who is still asking herself, 'Where are my parents?'

*'I was 10 when they were killed in a car crash, and I still think of them as Mummy and Daddy.'*

Mandy

She was told about their death at boarding school and she later overheard staff talking of their concern about what would happen to her.

Mandy said that she remembers that the days went by in a blur and she was given tranquillisers before and after the funeral. She did not cry, because she felt if she did, then so would everybody else. Mandy stayed silent. Her memory of that time is of a hush that would come over a room if she entered it and no-one – no-one at all – spoke to her about her parents. She never saw her home again. Holidays were usually spent with friends of her parents, who were kind but silent about the tragedy. Occasionally, she stayed with parents of a school friend. As Mandy grew up she felt she missed her mother more, especially at times such as the start of menstruation, dating or when she had a baby. Sex became a way of receiving affection and closeness and Mandy was married early to a man in his 40s. She had found a father, but her search for a mother continued until she went into therapy. It was then, and only then, that she could allow herself to remember and to speak about the bad times, and to cry for her parents. She found it unbearably sad to realise that all the adults around her had kept silent in the mistaken idea that they were helping her to forget and that if they spoke of her parents they might upset her. Mandy remembers that her mother used a certain scent and as a girl she used to go to a department store and stand around the perfume counter to breath in the smell of her mother. Mandy felt that was all she had.

> *'If a child loses a parent, for whatever reason, please tell their carers to help the child to keep that parent alive in their memory. Even if a child sees a father each weekend, during the week that man is lost to the child for the other six days.'*

Mandy

Mandy had felt for years she had been stuck around the age of 10 and that the affair she had begun recently was part of a very late adolescent rebellion. She shocked all her friends and family by announcing she wanted to be known as Amanda – a name she felt was more suited to her age than that of the 10-year-old Mandy.

## CHILDREN MOURNING

Children mourn in a different way from adults and although there may be periods where they appear to have forgotten their distress, it can surface again over the course of their development and as they mature. The saying, 'children are as tough as old boots', is to help adults to protect themselves by cutting off from children's distress. Children cannot always find words for their intense feelings but the belief that they are resilient and bounce back is cruel fiction. Even an infant who cannot comprehend what is happening senses a great deal.

# Chapter 12
# *Fathers Speak Back*

---

'It is seldom indeed that one parts on good terms:
because if one were on good terms one would not
part.'

MARCEL PROUST

'One man, one wife, one love through life –.'
Popular 1950s song

W<sub>E HAVE</sub> heard mostly from mothers so far. In this chapter, we hear more from fathers about their views of the effects of divorce and separation.

'Many people think that a divorce is the end but with children involved how can it be?'

Alan

So what is it like to be a non-custodial parent? This book is not intended to be an attack on fathers; we have told the stories as they were told to us. But, whatever the feelings of the adults, and however friendly are the arrangements made by the parents, the children will still ask questions that need answering.

## TELLING THE CHILDREN
'When I was going, I told the children (18 and 20) that mother and I could not live together because we didn't get on and that we hoped to get on better when we lived apart and that we both loved them.'

Tom

*'The main question my children asked when I told them I was leaving was where would I live and when would they see me after I left?'*

Adrian

*'I did it all wrong – I left without talking to my kids. I think I just mentally crossed my fingers and hoped they'd be OK. I trusted my ex-wife. The first weekend I had them after the separation I introduced them to the girl who was to become my wife. Too soon, much too soon.'*

Bernie

*'I just knew I wanted out of my marriage and it wasn't long after that I began an affair with my assistant, Julie. My wife found out, which speeded up my leaving home and moving in with Julie. After my divorce, I certainly didn't want to rush into a second marriage but Julie did, so we married. Actually, just before the wedding I began an affair with Rosie – I really fell in love. My marriage to Julie only lasted six months and I am very happy now with Rosie. I suppose my children did ask "Where's Daddy?". I didn't help them with the answer – I didn't know where I was myself for a couple of years.'*

Ron

## THE EFFECTS ON THE CHILDREN

Jeff described the very stormy relationship he had had with his partner and how he believed that it was not right to bring up the children in such a battling home. He left only after years of 'trying again'. No third person was involved. He considered very seriously trying to stay until the children were older, but this proved to be impossible. The arrangements for access were agreed and kept to, but over the years Jeff began to realise just how much he was missing out on the upbringing of his children.

*'It's the day-to-day chatter of kids . . . when they mention Miss This or Miss That I have to say who's that? I am only a visitor in their lives, and I've got to live with that. I get very lonely and I do*

*try not to let them see that. God knows it's not their fault we split.'*

Jeff

He considered all our questions carefully and tried to give an honest answer. He was shocked to read the question asking how he felt the separation affected the children. After thinking hard, he told us that Shirley (13) did have problems with eating and he decided to talk directly to his ex-wife about this. Up to then he had dismissed it in his mind as a teenage thing, but now he wanted to discuss with his former partner whether or not they should be concerned over Shirley's weight and perhaps get her some help. Jeff also thought he would take some time to discuss other questions in our list directly with his daughter.

*'After all, I left because I thought it was best for us all; I don't want to mess it up now by not answering their questions.'*

Jeff

Barry, a successful businessman in his late 40s, talked about what he remembered of the time he left his wife with three daughters under 10.

*'You might think I was a rat, but I realised there were other things to do, and places to go. I couldn't get caught up in all that childcare stuff like Maureen.'*

Barry

He found no difficulty in telling us that he told his ex-wife he was leaving and wanted a divorce but that he would support her and the children financially. He said that there were other changes in their lives: they had to move to a much smaller house quite quickly and consequently change schools. Barry was convinced that the children had come to no harm as a result of his leaving, and the fact that Maureen was subsequently treated for clinical depression seemed, to him, to be quite irrelevant. When asked how much contact he had with the children he replied:

*'Not a lot really. Young children are better off with their mothers and anyway I hadn't left home in order to become one of those fathers you see dragging around the park on a Sunday, not my scene.'*

Barry

He firmly believed the children just got on with growing-up and, 'had plenty of other adults around them.' Meanwhile he was free to get on with the very different life he wanted. All the children are in their late teens now and if he's in the country, he might meet with one of them for dinner occasionally. Barry says he feels he has had a good life and has no regrets.

Al, a man now in his late 50s, remembered how he felt when leaving his wife and two small children. This happened 25 years ago, but he can still recall the pain of hearing his elder daughter (2½ years old) saying as he left, 'Daddy, you're very sorry with Mummy aren't you?' Al felt the children learnt about the separation 'through its happening', and he told them nothing at the time. Although his family thought he had done the right thing, he had to cope with the shock/horror reaction of friends and colleagues. Later, his elder daughter asked, 'Do you love me, Dad?' and he replied, 'I love you more than I can say.' Years on she told him she was convinced that he did not love her, and Al still finds that very harrowing to remember.

William told us that although he left the marriage, it was after much thought and many discussions with his ex-wife. At the time, no-one else was involved but shortly after leaving he did meet – and move in with – a colleague.

*'I was sad about leaving Norma; she was only 5 at the time. I told her again and again it's about married couples divorcing, but parents never divorce their children. My wife said the same to Norma. However, Norma did suffer, and I know she missed me a lot. When I took her back to her mum on a Sunday afternoon, Norma would begin to cry, and sometimes so did I. I used to put some of my aftershave on her Teddy's face and I told her she could kiss her Teddy at night and the smell would make her feel close to*

*me. One day Norma came out with her Teddy, which had an arm missing and when I asked her how the accident happened, she replied, "I twisted it off." That was the first time I realised Norma was angry as well as sad. Your question, "Doesn't he [Daddy] love me any more?" was the one which choked me. I know from my ex-wife that Norma does ask that and I do trust her to reply "of course he does". Actions speak louder than words and I do fear Norma will see my leaving as not loving – whatever I do. I'd do anything to put the clock back.'*

William

*'I think we got it right. I waited until my daughter left for university and then I told my wife I wanted a change. I hadn't wanted my daughter to see us upset and rowing. I decided to spend two nights a week away from home, and got a small flat.'*

George

They have two boys, aged 15 and 13, and George said that they are not at all affected; they have no idea what is going on. We asked more about the boys, and George reluctantly volunteered the information that the youngest has trouble sleeping but George feels this is in no way connected to his behaviour. His wife agrees that they should keep quiet about what is happening. We were curious about what really is happening, and George then told us he spends the two nights a week with his mistress. We wondered whether his wife 'knows' on one level, but is colluding with him not to rock the boat, perhaps for reasons of her own.

When Chris saw our questionnaire at first he thought of it in the light of his own children who he sees for one week in the summer and for one week at Christmas. Then he thought of it in quite another way; he could 'hear' his own voice in his head, the voice of a 9-year-old boy asking, 'Where's Daddy?' again and again to a mother who would never give him a reply that satisfied him. As an adult, and father, he wonders now if she did reply as best she could but because it wasn't the answer he wanted, he continued to hear the replies as evasive and vague. Chris says he can remember that when he was a teenager he made a firm decision not to waste any more time trying to fathom out what had happened, and where his father was. In the calculated coldness of an adolescent he began to tell people, if they enquired, that his father was dead. It was only years later when his wife became pregnant that the first stirring of feelings and thoughts were apparent. He began to think about being a dad and all the old fantasies and dreams came back about his own father. 'Oh Dad, where are you?' became stronger after his daughter was born and even more pressing when, two years later, his wife gave birth to a son.

*'As the years went by I began to yearn for a dad in a way I never had before. I had no father inside me to call upon for reference, and I left the care of the kids to Pam. I'd see fathers on TV, but do real ones behave like that? I didn't know what to feel or do. Pam suggested I should see a counsellor, but I didn't see how one could help me. Looking back, though, I think she was right. What I did was to get involved with a woman I work with and once Pam found out about that I was out. I wonder if that is what happened to my father? My mother died several years ago and now I will never know what did happen. I suppose the only connection I have with my dad is that neither of us could be dads. Sometimes I wonder if it is too late – perhaps counselling could help me after all?'*

Chris

Charlie described for us the break-up of his marriage after 15 years. There are two children, who were 6 and 3 at the time of the separation. Charlie felt the changes had been well orchestrated and that as he moved to live close by the children had frequent contact with him. Access, we were told, was mutually agreed at the time of separation and was never a serious problem. Part of the preparation was arranged through a solicitor, and together with his wife he saw a mediator. Charlie also told us he later saw a counsellor and also consulted an educational psychologist when the eldest child developed a learning diffculty. He says that they did the best they could. That was 25 years ago, and Charlie said he saw no outward or inward sign of difficulties as his children moved into adolescence. Only now he observes, do his children as adults cause him concern.

> *'Neither are keen to marry and the youngest is over-sensitive to arguments of the mildest nature between me and my second wife. I am hoping they will both see a therapist – there must be things for them to sort out, I can't do it any more.'*

Charlie

## LATER REGRETS

Graham told us he married in his 20s and had two children. Graham's work kept him away from home, sometimes for weeks at a time. On one of these spells away he began a relationship with a colleague and within six months had left home and moved in with Sally. Graham was very troubled when he told us that access with his two children was sporadic and pretty unfulfilling. Time passed and he and Sally married and they had a daughter. This time Graham was very involved with Sally and with childcare. Only then did he begin to realise just what he had missed last time round, and although he tried hard to repair his relationship with his first two children, it was too late. As teenagers, they were remote and reproachful and had little inclination to spend time with their father and his new family. Graham now says he finds it hard to get out of his mind the sadness of the mistakes he made in his 20s. His remorse cuts no ice with his eldest children, and he feels it is a heartache he will have to carry for the rest of his life.

Roger read the text of this chapter as he was in the process of separating from his wife and family. His first and immediate comment was that not enough was written generally, or spoken about, of the pain around the break-up of a family. He found our manuscript sobering reading. Roger told us that several of his colleagues are married for the second time, and the word gets passed around – 'Old so-and-so has left his wife you know, gone off with the blond in PR', – and the conversation shifts to other topics. If old so-and-so is asked directly how things are the reply is likely to be 'OK – I still see the kids, and they love Rosy/Liz/or Kathy' and the conversation changes again. The pain of it all is glossed over and the myth goes on that partners can be changed without the apple cart being upset.

*'If I could, I'd turn the clock back, but I can't and I can only hope that the three of us (the adults) can explain the facts to the kids in a way that will cushion them from as much damage and hurt as possible. When I first began to chat up Maggie I had no idea what a tidal wave could and would hit us. Nobody told me to take care of what I had.'*

Roger

Jimmy told us that with hindsight he finds the memory of his divorce almost too much to bear when he thinks of the impact on his daughter, Lucy, then only 8 years old. Jimmy and his wife found it intolerable to live together – the arguments often went on long into the night, and he admits that Lucy was a spectator to much of this. Jimmy left, and to his subsequent chagrin left Lucy with her mother, thinking it would be best for her. Jimmy went to the Middle East to work and now he can understand that Lucy would have been left wondering 'Where's Daddy?'. Three years later he learnt that the relationship which his ex-wife had entered into had failed. In his concern for Lucy he returned to England to find that his ex-wife was in a psychiatric hospital because of a severe depression seemingly brought about by the collapse of the second marriage. Lucy was with an aunt and Jimmy found a very silent, withdrawn little girl, who flinched at any sudden or loud sound. Jimmy said he cannot forgive himself for leaving Lucy to go through yet another breakdown. He says he is facing Lucy's, 'Where's Mummy?', as he struggles to create a stable home for them both.

Jim felt he had a raw deal and said that although he knows his infidelity caused the split, he did still want to maintain contact with his child.

*'Every time I rang to speak to Ellie I was told it was too late or she was out, any old excuse.'*

Jim

He did take Ellie out some weekend days, but says he found it difficult to talk to a 6-year-old. He let the contact drop and says he meant to take it up again when she was older when it would be easier to go out for the day with her.

*'That was my big mistake. When Ellie got older she had no time for me and I think her mum had painted a pretty bad picture of me.'*

Jim

He wanted us to urge newly separated fathers to 'stick in there' and hold on to the relationship they had with a child, however fragile.

*'I'm not in a hurry to make the same mistakes again, and make myself and my children miserable. They deserve a lot better than they had, and so do I. It's better to be on my own with them than to be with the wrong woman.'*

Adam

*'My wife and I were both to blame – we were both involved with someone else. That's a very unhappy situation, but what is worse is that my daughter became a referee in our marriage and I can see that wasn't fair. She carried far too much. I am very sorry about that.'*

Tom

*'I was 35 when I began to feel quite desperate, that life was closing in on me. I told my then partner that I had to travel and no way could I take her and the kids with me. I had to get away, and I did. I went round the world and it wasn't till I got back I realised I'd gone on the wrong kind of journey. I'd had plenty of time to think and I realised I should have gone into therapy, to sort things out. I tried to go back home and said I'd go to therapy, but she wouldn't give me a second chance. She won't let me see the kids.'*

Clive

# CONTACT

*'Access was mutually agreed at the time of separation. It was never a serious problem – except the wife occasionally felt I saw too much of them and it interfered with her plans of life for them.'*

Sebastian

*'The hardest thing for me is seeing my children so upset. All my life I have felt pulled in two directions. I could never settle to anything or anyone. Three years in therapy is helping me to link those feelings to the break-up of my parents' relationship when I was 7. My father went to France to live and I found it almost impossible to move between Mum and Dad. I find it unbelievable that my children are now going through what I experienced.'*

Leo

*'No one even missed me. The day I moved out my mother-in-law moved in – I haven't been back.'*

Gordon

Brian suggested that for many fathers the real sticking point is how to share out the children for Christmas and birthdays. He said that he suggested to his ex-partner that they ask the children (Phil, 8, and Kay, 9) what they want.

*'I can't stand the idea of not seeing the children on their birthdays – I left my wife, but not my kids.'*

Brian

He then told us that his ex-partner (Phoebe) felt it was an unfair burden to put on the children as they would be put in the position of choosing one parent over another. She maintains that the separation was not of the children's making; this is their problem and they should sort it out. Brian told us he feels this is just talk on Phoebe's part, and that she is afraid to put the idea to the children in case they chose to spend a very special day with him and not with their mother. To us, this seemed to be an extension of the discord between Brian and Phoebe, and in fact the needs of the children were not being considered.

Another couple (the Shaws); faced with a similar problem over holidays and birthdays, sorted the situation out by these steps: they met together without the children to rough out a plan of holidays and birthdays; when general agreement had been reached they met as a family to put to the children (all in their teens) the plan they had drafted as parents (not as a couple at war). For this family, this system worked well. The children felt free to chip in with their comments – it was the children who said it was fun to spend more of the Easter break with Dad, because he will probably take them camping, but they preferred to spend more of Christmas with their Mum and her parents because that is what they have done every Christmas of their lives. To use the familiarity of 'before the divorce' is a good way of maintaining some certainty and stability in a family at a time of so many other changes.

The Shaws hoped to avoid any direct or indirect pressure on the children, and felt they had managed to avoid the pitfall of competition between parents. It appears that the children were able to pick up that their parents genuinely had their best interest at heart, and this gave them the freedom to say they enjoyed camping with Dad and Christmas with Mum at Gran's, without feeling they were wounding one of their parents. Mr and Mrs Shaw said they both felt the children's self-esteem had probably been rocked by the break-up of the family and they felt by including them in the discussions they were demonstrating to their children that they still had parents and that their views were respected.

> 'As a father, I get a very bad reaction for having resident shared care of my girls, aged 6 and 9 years. I can feel people thinking that I must be peculiar and how terrible it is that I take them away from their mother, because that is the place for two girls growing up, isn't it? If my ex-wife wants to change arrangements I always ask myself "What's in it for me?". I know that sounds selfish but people are always going to criticise me whatever I do regarding the girls, and not understand me not wanting to let go, and so I may as well do what I feel is right.'
>
> Michael

*'Do I see my girls regularly? I'll say I do. Every week there seems to be something they need me to buy. I'm a soft touch where they are concerned so they both get what they want. They also know that if they tell me their mother won't get them new boots, I will.'*

Stan

## A RAW DEAL?

Some men feel that they have a raw deal with the law and society all being on the side of the women and children.

It is an ugly fact that many fathers won't pay maintenance unless they are allowed to see their children. Despite the Child Support Agency, the battle of access v maintenance continues – at a high cost to all concerned. Each year, 150,000 children lose contact with their non-custodial parent (code for father), according to the organisation Families Need Fathers. This organisation urges a change of culture whereby it becomes as socially unacceptable to stop access as not to pay maintenance.

*'I was difficult over maintenance in the case of my own child after my marriage broke down. But now that access has been sorted out I don't mind paying. I should have paid but I was angry.'*

Billy

*'I see my two boys, now 15 and 17, on a regular basis even though we are 250 miles apart. I am lucky that I have the money and time to be able to make this possible.'*

Steven

*'I left Sue and little John (almost 2 years old) to live with a girl I had met. This didn't last, but my wife would not hear of us trying to work things out after that. She then used her power as mother to move to Ireland without my consent but what could I do? I don't drive and to see my son is a major expense that I just cannot afford more than once a month. What kind of relationship can I have with my son now? There was no reason for her to move so far away from Canterbury but she did. Poor John, and poor me.'*

Martin

'We were divorced nine years ago and I do see Beth (15) one weekend a month. That's a good time for me, and I hope for her too. I don't have any photos of her as a baby, or as a little girl, and my ex-wife won't let me have any. It's as if part of my life has been wiped out.'

John

'I expected a battle when I left my wife and baby, but not a drawn-out war. It's five years now, but she is still difficult if I want things from the home – my tools for instance. She makes me feel I'm a crook if I ask for anything, even our photograph album.'

Bill

'Thirty years on my daughters have never forgiven me for leaving their mother. They hate the woman I love and married, and the strain has nearly killed me. I have had three heart attacks.'

Neil

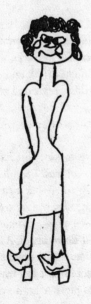 

# Chapter 13
# *The Future*

'Fill the cup that clears
Today of past regrets and future fears.'
 EDWARD FITZGERALD, *The Rubáiyát of Omar Khayyám*

'A woman's career, particularly if it is successful, is
often blamed for the break-up of a marriage, but
never a man's.'

EVA FIGES

So HE'S gone after all and now it's you and the children.
What next?

'I just can't believe he's done it; what a relief to us all. Perhaps now
the children and I can get on with our lives. The children won't go
to bed wondering if he will come home tonight drunk and cause a
screaming row. I can double lock the front door, relax and go to bed
in peace.'

Sally

'I've no idea what to do now; my life seems to have lost half of its
purpose. Thank goodness for the children – at least I can look like
I'm coping and getting on with it all.'

Sandra

'Every time I build up my life he knocks it down again. A change
with contact, cutting down on maintenance – it is always something. And this is four years after my divorce. When can my future
begin?'

Connie

The lull after the storm is, for many women, a time of numbness and indecision and it is probably best for everyone involved if no major decisions have to be made at this time.

*'I knew we would have to move house at some point, because it was too big and I wasn't receiving enough financial support from my ex-partner to cover the running costs. I held off moving because I didn't know where I wanted to move to, back North to be with my family or locally. I was fortunate to be able to stand still and not even try to make the choice for 18 months until me and the children could decide what was best for us all. When we finally did move back from where we'd come, it was a huge success because we had taken our time to plan for it and all looked forward to it together, seeing the move as a new beginning.'*

Sue

*'I dreaded my husband leaving me; it was the worst fear of my life. I thought I would die if he ever left me: I thought I'd be unable to cope without his support. I never went to sleep at night until he was home safely, even as it got later and later. Usually I didn't know where he was or why he was so late, I worried and worried. Then one night I needed sleep so badly, was so stressed out, I realised I needed to break free from my terrible dread. Needing to protect myself, I started thinking OK so the car crashes, he dies and then what? I realised the more I thought this through it didn't seem as dreadful as this state I was in. I knew I would cope, I could go on and it occurred to me that life might even be less stressful. When I look back I think I knew he was seeing someone else and this was the first bit of self-preservation I did for myself and the children.'*

Patricia

*'After Paul went it took me a long, long time to realise I had a future – or rather that I could have one if I worked at leaving the past behind. Eventually, I started to date and invited him to dinner. It was then I realised, with horror, that three years after Paul left I was so used to cooking mince and chicken nuggets I had almost completely forgotten how to cook a sophisticated adult meal.*

*I rang my sister and her husband and made them come for a practice dinner and I served them up an elegant candlelit meal. Only then did I have the confidence to invite Jim home.'*

Elizabeth

Some women embark on a rediscovery of themselves, taking control of their happiness and being responsible for it, in a way not realised before. It could also perhaps mean starting to date men immediately after the break-up. This can often be for the wrong reasons.

## NEW FRIENDS AND RELATIONSHIPS

*'I went straight into another relationship when my ex left, because to have a new partner and to feel wanted and to be taken out was the only way I knew how to show the world and my ex he hadn't destroyed me. I soon realised that I was mad to try and fill my life with a man who I didn't like much, let alone love, and decided to go it alone. I tried to fill the emptiness inside with positive understanding and concentrated on making myself feel good about myself alone. It is hard suddenly to be only half a partnership, but once I had realised that didn't mean I was half a person, I got on a lot better.'*

Maggie

*'I found that it is a real turning point to recovery when you can concentrate on yourself and your future, not the break-up of the relationship and your ex-partner. I felt at last I was not thinking of John all the time and stopped asking the question 'Why?' all the time, and realised that I was on the road to recovery with a positive outlook.'*

Julie

*'My life took on a new direction when I woke one morning and decided to look for support where I would receive it, and not waste time and energy just wishing him back.'*

Kate

'I started saying yes to every social engagement I was asked to, even if it was the PTA school quiz evening. One such evening I had spent half the time glaring at the husbands thinking how good Barrie would have been at answering the questions and how much he would have enjoyed it. Then I came home, paid the babysitter, and sat at the kitchen table and cried and cried as if my heart would break. I said out loud, "I don't want to be free and single, and having to start again with everything." I liked being married: I had felt safe, secure, happy and thought I knew where I was going – everything now is such hard work, and I feel so very tired and fragile.'

Angela

'I'm not really ready to think of the future. Sometimes I think I am and then something happens that knocks me back. I was divorced three years ago, yet one evening last week I was let down by a woman friend for a social evening. I put down the telephone and just cried for hours. When I asked myself why it was, I realised it was because I was lonely. When I'd been married I had a dull social life – but then I was at home with three children under 3 so what did I expect? I think that is the real problem I am facing – I expect now a "better" life, more fun and happier and it's not happened yet.'

Alice

'I can't see the future yet. But I do make lists of things of what I'll do one day.'

Penny

'A new relationship was the very last thing on my mind. I decided very early on to give myself wholeheartedly to the children for that first year after the separation. I always put their needs and emotions first. I wasn't being hard on myself, as there was nothing in particular that I wanted to do anyway. This also gave me time and space for thought, without the pressures of doing "the right thing for the future" before I was ready to do anything.'

Sandra

As Sandra found, it is possible to prolong the stages of recovery, whether consciously or subconsciously, and to delay the new start and the hard work and effort it takes to get on with it. It is very frightening, albeit exciting at times, to some women to initiate a social evening on their own, or to start applying for jobs, after being at home for several years. Other women wait until they feel strong enough for another knock or let down before they even contemplate trying something new.

Making new friends can be hard, especially if you are not happy with your new single position. Do you say, 'Hi, I'm divorced with three children', or talk generally and then slip it into the conversation at a later time? It can almost be a relief to be divorced because it is often so hard to say you are separated.

*'Separation is such a no-man's-land state to be in — no-one knew what that really meant did it mean that I had had a row with my partner that weekend or was I just not quite actually divorced?'*

Janey

Lily told us she had been very hurt hearing from friends of hers and her ex-husband's all about his new girlfriend who had been there at dinner the last week:

*'I had seen Pip and May many times over the past year with the girls, who are the same ages as their two girls, and hearing how they had been to dinner and I had only been asked to teas, made me feel like a second-class citizen.'*

Lily

*'Over the past couple of years I veered away from friends who had known us both as a couple. I wanted new friends who could meet me how I am now, not as half an old couple. I think this is the healthy way, and anyway after Luke went, some friends I saw who had known us together only wanted to talk about that, and it was the one topic of conversation I was trying to put behind me. It was just something that got referred to again and again in the old circle of friends.'*

Kate

*'I joined a couple of these singles clubs because I wanted to meet people who hadn't known me with Paul. But after several attempts I realised this was a very false set-up, and also so women-heavy that it made me feel rather cheap. As I was trying to up my image and confidence I stopped going.'*

Jo

*'I was desperate to make new friends. I went straight out the next week and got a part-time job in the local bakery. I didn't care what the job was as long as it gave me a different place than the home to be in and got me communicating with people.'*

Kate

If your children are young and at school, there are always plenty of other women around for a chat. Women joined clubs, such as a working women's group, Gingerbread, or the National Women's Register, or alternatively local gyms or tennis clubs. A good way to meet people is to volunteer to help locally in the community; this may lead to new interests as well as new people.

## MAKING OTHER CHANGES

Some women make physical changes to themselves, for example dramatically changing their hair or clothes.

*'I had to change something and quickly because I felt so very different inside and I also thought that people looking at me expected to see some change and evidence of what I'd been through, apart from the red eyes of course!'*

Sue

*'My ex-husband always made a terrible fuss if I wore anything black – in fact he wouldn't allow it. Guess what now? I dress in black from head to toe every single day, I love it and feel great.'*

Kay

Julie decided to tackle her fear:

*'I was terrified about ill health or accidents in the home. Now I was on my own with the children, especially at night, I worried*

*constantly that if something happened to one of the boys I wouldn't know what to do. After a couple of months of worrying about this, I decided to do something positive, and found out about local first aid courses. My neighbour agreed to babysit in the evenings and I went for it. When 19 weeks later I achieved my certificate, I felt great and confident in my ability, should it be put to the test. I felt happier with myself. I had even met a couple of new friends who I would keep in touch with now the course was over.'*

Julie

# CAREERS, TRAINING AND INTERESTS

*'I thought I'd go straight back to work after Mark left me and my two pre-school aged kids, and I was lucky that the hospital where I got work had a crèche. Polly was in the baby crèche and Billy was in the nursery. It was a pity they couldn't be together, but that was the way it was. I would drop them off before breakfast and pick them up after work at about a quarter to six. This went on for a year before my mother thought that perhaps the terrible times I was having in the stressful evenings and weekends were down to this way of "sort of non-family-life" that I was having with them. They wouldn't sleep at night and Billy would not get interested in the potty, not to mention the frequent tantrums. When we did spend a day together, I found I was too tired to give them much love and attention. I was made to consider that maybe the situation was not working as well as I thought, and it was terrible, because I had no choice. I couldn't afford a nanny or mother's help, and my family were down in Exeter. And so the situation went on and on and I convinced myself that it was for the best after all and that they would grow out of their difficult phase.'*

Lorraine

The organisations Wel-Care and Gingerbread are both devoted to supporting single parents and can often help to make contact with local women's groups. There is some comfort to be had from contact with other women who are either in the same boat or who have been through a similar desperate time.

*'Several years ago I worked for Wel-Care as a social worker and during that time met many girls and young women who were on their own, either pregnant or struggling to bring up a child single-handed. Even the bravest and strongest of them needed some support. Perhaps we played — in Winnicott terms — the part of the father at times in order to allow the mother the space to care for her child.'*

Jill

Women answered our questionnaire saying that their main aim for the future was, 'to get my life back', 'to have a good future' and 'to be in control of my destiny'. Women looking on the bright side of the separation saw it, amongst other things, as giving them a second chance at a career, either a new one or one put on hold while the children were growing up. This opportunity would not have arisen had the marriage continued, and so with hindsight these women are thankful!

*'I now have a full-time responsible job I could not have held if still married.'*

Laura

*'Over the last 12 years since the separation, my career has blossomed in a way which satisfies me. I know this would not have happened if I had remained in the relationship.'*

Margaret

Women answering our questionnaire whose children were at school full-time seemed keen to use the time now to take up a subject of interest to them and many embarked on further education courses. These varied from painting classes to degrees and diplomas, in new fields as well as refresher development career courses, to widen their horizons. This was seen as an exciting time of living again after a period for many of merely existing.

But for the hundreds of women working at the time of the separation, it meant in reality that they had to work longer hours, or go full-time from part-time. This often meant taking on some kind of extra help such as childcare, perhaps leaving the children for longer hours at a time when they needed their mother more. What choice is there if it is the difference between keeping the house and putting food on the table or a much lower standard of living? Men who left wives and children were not always forthcoming with financial support. Repeatedly we were told of women who had to earn money and find work – any work – immediately. This is not an easy thing to do at a time when self confidence is low and fears and anxieties are high.

*'I want to retrain in a field which will give me greater working satisfaction than I've had in the past.'*

Pat

One subject mentioned on many forms was, 'training to be a counsellor'. Perhaps out of the suffering has come the realisation that although life cannot be the same again, experience has been gained; many women want to be in a position to use this knowledge to help others.

*'I'm afraid the enclosed is rather unsatisfactory. I found it very painful – largely because I was not aware enough of the children – I did my psychotherapy course much later, and became aware that we hadn't observed them enough.'*

Suzanne

*'My main aim in life after Peter went was to earn a decent living – somehow!'*

Philippa

Returning to work is not always easy for a mother: the holidays are long, children are ill, nannies can be off sick and all this makes an employer feel he was right not to employ a 'mother' before, and he certainly won't again.

*'I need to get out more and perhaps do a course. But I can't pay for*

*anything, and would love to have a job but I wouldn't be able to pay all the bills.'*

Elsie

*'I am endeavouring to find a better paid and more secure job, now that my youngest is at full-time school.'*

Carrie

*'I was the main breadwinner before my husband left, so I suffered no financial hardship as a result of the break-up. The emotional hardship was another matter, but I did have a career which was satisfying.'*

Jane

# FEELINGS ABOUT THE FUTURE

We did hear of women with positive views of the future, but we also heard from women who are still cowed by loss of self-esteem and struggle each day with the loneliness and fear of what the future will bring. Often this was shadowed by lack of financial security and anxiety about paying the bills.

*'I'd like to be able to learn something, get a good job and to bring up the children as best I can. I don't know if the first is possible without money.'*

Jackie

*'I can't see ahead. I am too busy trying to get through today. Jeff has stopped seeing our son (who is 12) – he doesn't want to upset his new girlfriend – and at the same time has stopped paying any maintenance. He just wants us out of his life. How can he live the rest of his life knowing he has a son he never sees? Not a day goes by when I don't worry about the long-term effects on my little boy.'*

Esther

*'I almost made a go of a new relationship, but I was so insecure that it all fell apart.'*

Deb

*'I am so lonely and I have this awful feeling that I would lose it all over again even if I did find the right man.'*

Rosie

*'Everyone says I'm young and pretty and will marry again. They don't understand that sometimes I still feel I'm dying inside. I wish I didn't still love him, but I do. I still long to give him a cuddle, but he's no longer mine. I hope he finds out one day what it's like to be lonely.'*

Sarah

*'I have been on my own for six years and I feel at my lowest ebb now. I am so lonely. I have had partners I didn't even like just for company. I now don't want to do that any more, but panic is overwhelming me. I am afraid of the future – I'm locking myself into the past.'*

Ali

*'I may be 40, but over the last five years I have needed my mum and dad more than at any other time in my life. I hurt so much.'*

Antonia

*'I don't hate my ex-partner now. I feel he did what he did out of desperation. Acknowledging that has set me free.'*

Sally

*'Five years on, the boys and I are happily getting on with our lives. I want people to know that broken hearts can heal and life can be joyful again.'*

Daphne

*'I intend to take more holidays, go on a higher degree course and try to make up for the years I have lost.'*

Sara

# CONCLUSION

Not surprisingly, although some women are able to stride into the future, others find it difficult to build a bridge between their old and new lives. Perhaps the difference is between those who have been able to 'wash the man right out of their hair' and those who still feel entangled and enmmeshed emotionally with their former partner. Certainly, where there are arrangements to be made about children, the untangling and bitterness can prevent the future being seen in a positive light.

> 'Eighteen years after our divorce we are still fighting over who should give our son a celebration lunch after his graduation.'
>
> Lily

> 'In the words of the song by Barry Manilow – "I'm doing OK but not very well".'
>
> Paula

> 'Don't wait for your boat to come in but swim out to meet it.'
>
> Tessa

I movd to LONDON and I movd to a new SCHOOl I am HAPPY There

# Chapter 14
# *The Final Word*

---

*'Love is sweet for a day, but love grows bitter with treason.'*

SWINBURNE

WHAT HAVE we learnt from women (and men) who have been through separation as parents? We have heard that for many it was never straightforward to understand that the relationship was at an end. However rocky a partnership is, the untangling of it is difficult, complicated and often very painful. The hurt of earlier losses can be remembered and felt again. Everyone carries into adulthood a child's fear of being left alone and unprovided for, and this fear can surface at this time.

This is a period when friends and family should rally round. Some friends are able to do this, but others may become wary, as if pain can be contagious. Anxiety can run high. After all, if it could happen to you it could happen to anyone. For those with family support – not everyone has a close extended family – this can be a blessing for the back-up they provide. However, the pain and anger felt on your behalf by some siblings and parents can also be an additional burden.

The reason for the break-up can be a contributing factor to the unhappiness. Although our research was initially intended only to cover the questions children ask when a marriage ends through divorce, we soon became embroiled in questions about the loss of a father for other reasons; death and imprisonment are two of the other issues we addressed.

The statistics at the beginning of the book provide details of the number of children affected by divorce. They do not cover other relationships which have broken up – these are not recorded. But perhaps binding relationships are no longer the norm. This was highlighted recently in a nostalgic article in *The Sunday Times* on the 60s by A.A.Gill, who spoke eloquently of, 'the time when parents came in pairs'.

The loss of a parent during childhood – for whatever reason – is one of the most stressful events an individual can face. As the research by Dr Martin Richards shows, children are affected by divorce, and no class or gender is spared. To a child the fact that a parent chose to leave attacks his or her self-esteem. A sense of abandonment can haunt a child into adulthood, which can mean that they may enter too rapidly into a relationship in which they are potentially vulnerable at an early age. The psychologist John Bowlby believed a child's earlier patterns of attachment and loss determined his or her resilience or vulnerability to later stressful lives. The stability of the resident parent is of paramount importance if the child is to weather the loss with minimum stress.

As we have seen, children are often the first to know that there are problems within the parental relationship. Frequently, because of their immaturity, they are not able to verbalise their anxieties and often they have to find another way to communicate. For very young children this may be by becoming clinging, wetting or soiling again, or by otherwise regressing in their behaviour to an earlier stage of development. Children who are a little older may react by developing problems when separating from the resident parent, for example, at the time they start school or on access visits to the other parent. Schoolwork may well suffer at this time.

Adolescents are more likely to show their anxiety and stress by behaviour problems or mood swings. At a time when they are learning about adult relationships they see the most important relationship in their lives falling apart.

Adult children are certainly not left untouched by their parents' divorce. Young adults beginning to live their own separate lives seem especially vulnerable. However independent someone feels it is part of the stability within oneself to know, unconsciously, that parents are somewhere in the background if needed.

We have seen how eating problems and difficulty with sleep can surface during any of these stages.

In addition to being upset by the parental break-up, children are also stressed by other changes that occur around the same time. Remembering her own father leaving when she was 8, Emily can now only recall that her beloved dog went with him; the rest is a blur. She says she still grieves for that pet, and she is shocked at how little she can recall of the other changes which took place then.

The pain of a break-up often affects a wide circle of family and friends. We have learnt that other children in the extended family become concerned. Sammy – aged 4 – decided that Grandpa must be his cousin's daddy. Once he had put that into place in his mind he seemed less worried about the sudden absence of an uncle. We know of children who worry when friends' parents separate – and they too asked questions.

Parents were honest in telling us that although logically and in retrospect, they would have liked to answer their children's questions in a clear unbiased way, in reality emotions frequently coloured the replies.

*'If I had my time over again there is one thing I would change. I did discourage phone calls in the beginning. Tom and Alice would hear me upset on the phone to my ex so when he asked to speak to them they would not want to come to the phone and speak to their father. I'm sorry about that – it didn't help the children.'*

Kathy

Handover from one parent to another seemed a time of great strain for many families. We hear from Maureen that by the time she was 8 she was missing Monday morning school because of the strain of the weekend, which would also bring on her sister's migraine.

From grown-up children, the memories of the time when their parents broke up were often sad for them to recall. Many spoke of their awareness of making sure they do not sabotage their present relationships through a constant anxiety of being abandoned.

*'I never want to divorce – and that means I'm afraid to marry.'*
Angela

From adults who had been children at the time of the break-up we frequently heard that no-one told them what was happening. Perhaps Chris partly explained this when he said he did ask, 'Where's Daddy?' again and again, but the answers didn't satisfy him because they were not the answers he wanted.

Some parents certainly hoped that a lot of what was happening went over the children's heads. This was not because they wanted to avoid their children's questions, but it was in the hope that the children would just get on with their lives and not be too affected by the situation. Some mothers (and fathers) did tell us that they did not explain in detail what was happening because they found it too painful to put the facts into words.

We hope that the more aware we all are of the strain on children when parents disagree or part, the more we can protect the children. Not by silence but by listening to and answering their questions, both spoken and unspoken, in a way which is informative and helpful. Seven-year old Lizzy when hearing we were writing this book said, 'I know quite a lot about divorce don't I?' Unfortunately, she did.

Some parents could, either together or separately, tell their children some of the facts.

*'We told the children together that once we loved each other very much, now we didn't.'*

Brian

In families where the atmosphere has been strained, the children have some warning. It is in families where feelings have been repressed and there has been no warning that shock becomes a greater part of the trauma. Children do need to experience some of the pain which their parents suffer. If they are totally shielded from this they can become bemused as to why their parents are separating.

215

*'My parents never had a cross word in front of us. I couldn't understand why they suddenly said they couldn't live together. The divorce was so friendly. My brother and I found it all so awful, and tantalizing. Why was this happy family splitting up? We didn't dare ask.'*

Eleanor

We have learnt of the different ways in which families have coped with the break-up of a relationship. What shall we tell the children? If the women who contacted us could speak with one voice we believe they would say, 'I'd listen to the children and try to answer their questions immediately, directly and simply. I would try not to colour my answers with my own pain and fear and sense of betrayal.' We also feel they would then go on to add, 'But I'm human and I was in pain and at times I floundered and panicked. I also, at times, tried to punish my ex-partner through the children.' Perhaps these things balance out, and as the new family settles and reorganises, the thing to remember is that questions come again and again from children, so new and clearer answers can be found. Ask yourself why you are answering a question in a certain way. If the answer is truly because it is best for the children, then say what is in your heart.

# Appendix I
# *The Questionnaire*

---

Some people filled in our questionnaire briefly and to the point. Others wanted to include much more information and detail than we gave space for, although some questions were deliberately open-ended so those replying could answer as fully as they felt inclined to.

A few questionnaires were returned to us partly completed, two with the following comments:

*'I really thought I would enjoy filling it in, but I'm afraid it brought back such unpleasant memories that I could not bring myself to go through the questions the children asked and to remember what I said. They did ask all those questions, but I was in such a state at the time I'm not sure I would want to tell you how I answered them even if I could force myself to remember.'*

Suzanne

*'Sorry it's not complete, but it happened three years ago and it's all a horrible haze. I don't think that at the time I did take much notice of the kids; I was in too much pain. I do remember a terrible row with Leo one night and the door opened and Gary stood there staring at us. I know I screamed, "Get out – go to bed", and he fled, white-faced, back to bed. I can't fit that in to your questionnaire, but it happened.'*

Carolyn (mother of Gary, 48)

Other comments were:

*'The divorced mother is not a person. There are single women,*

*single mothers, career women and wives. The divorced mother is seen as a threat by other women and as a failure or a push-over by other men. Big deal.'*

Paula

*'I've completed the questionnaire but you didn't leave enough space for me to fill in Q. 21 in detail. ("Was there physical violence witnessed by the children?") I have replied "yes" but perhaps you do need to know about the time Mark, then 2½, and Susie, then 4, saw me knocked flying across the kitchen – or the time they saw me dragged up the stairs by my hair? I could go on . . . The next question asks how the children reacted at a) home b) school c) as young adults? The brief answer is a) terrified b) withdrawn and c) very depressed. Mark is a heroin addict.'*

Fay

*'There were other questions you should have asked – where should I have put in my experience? I was having tea with my two who were 12 and 13 when my ex came in – drunk – and said "Guess what? I'm HIV positive". Do you call that being told in "one fell swoop"? (Q.27) The questions my children asked were, "Who's Dad had sex with?" and "Will you get Aids?" and "Will you both die?".*

Bridget

*'Why no questions about cruelty to animals? The crunch came in our family when my husband kicked our pregnant cat out of the way. The children saw him do that and I couldn't stand by and let them grow up believing that was a way to behave. That incident came on top of a lot of others, of course . . . We're divorced now.'*

Corrine

Amelia wanted us to know she showed our questionnaire to a friend who was on the verge of separating from her husband. Amelia repeated that her friend Marie took a very long time to read the questions and then confided that she had been attempting to answer the questions in her head – especially taking the part of her 7-year-old little boy. Amelia reports her friend saying:

*'I must find another way. If our kid is going to worry about all this if we split up, I must give Relate another try . . .'*

Amelia suggested that our questionnaire should be available for all engaged or married couples! Her experience with her friend made Amelia think that anything that encouraged the thought that marriages are not to be entered into or dissolved lightly should be widely circulated.

*'Jackie and I are still together, probably because of the kids. I read your questionnaire and we don't seem to fit into it. We are not separated or divorced but we do threaten each other with it. I wonder if that frightens the boys? When I get fed up I do sometimes shout, "That's it, I'm off and not coming back", and storm off to Jackie shouting, "Good". Would the kids believe we don't love them? It's got nothing to do with them, really.'*

Tony

These comments, all shocking in themselves, reinforce for us the fact that so many couples go through terrible pain when a relationship goes wrong. As we said in our foreword, divorce hurts, and hurts more people than the immediate couple. Frequently post-scripts on the questionnaire were in this vein: 'Tell people how awful it is', 'It's not like the movies – how did Elizabeth Taylor go through this again and again?', 'I can't bear to think how much pain my pathetic affairs have caused' and 'If I'd read, *Where's Daddy?* five years ago I think I would have been able to reply today, "right here", instead of "I'll see you in a month, son."'

One questionnaire was returned – not completed – with this comment:

*'Jim left us, but came back, and then left again. I think he's coming back for one more try so I don't know if we're separated or not so I'm sorry I can't fill in "Where's Daddy?". I don't even know for sure myself where he is!'*

WHERE'S DADDY?

WHERE'S DADDY?

# QUESTIONNAIRE

This questionnaire is confidential and, as you are not giving us your name, any information will not be attributed to you. If necessary it will be disguised and identifying features changed.

1. Are you a mother [ ] or a father [ ]?
2. How many children do you have?
3. Age and sex of children: .... [m/f] .... [m/f] .... [m/f] .... [m/f] .... [m/f] .... [m/f]
4. What is your age? 20–29 [ ] 30–35 [ ] 36–46 [ ] 47+ [ ]
5. How old were you when you married? [ ] Your partner [ ]
6. What year were you married?
7. How long have you been separated/divorced?
8. At the time of the separation did you have any help with the children? [y/n] If yes, did any changes take place?
9. Were you employed at the time of the separation? [y/n]
   If yes, what changes have taken place?
   If no, what goals do you have for the future?
10. How soon did you consult a solicitor?
    Immediately [y/n] six months on [y/n] later [y/n]
11. Did this make the situation for you easier or more difficult? [y/n]
    In what way?
12. Did you suffer financially?
    Immediately [y/n] six months on [y/n] later [y/n]
13. Did you have to move house?
    Immediately [y/n] six months on [y/n] later [y/n]
14. Do you think the maintenance/settlement finally agreed was fair?
15. When did you realise there might be unresolvable problems in the relationship? After how many months or years?
16. Did you have children by then? [y/n]
17. If yes, at what point do you think the children first picked up that things were not right?

18. What makes you say that? Can you give an example?

19. Did they ask any direct questions? If yes, can you tell us what they said?

20. Did you and your partner . . .

    . . . argue with each other in front of the children? [y/n]

    . . . not speak to each other in front of the children? [y/n]

21. Was there physical violence witnessed by the children?

22. If yes to 20 or 21 how did the children react?

    [a]. . . . at home:

    [b]. . . . at school:

    [c]. . . . as young adults.

23. Did you talk your problems over with anyone within the children's hearing?

24. If yes, do you think the children were old enough to understand what was being spoken about? [y/n]

25. Did you speak of your worries and concerns to:
friend [y/n] mother [y/n] other family member [y/n]
child [y/n] clergy [y/n] counsellor [y/n]
GP [y/n] au pair/nanny [y/n]

26. How did the children learn about the separation?

27. Were they told in stages or one fell swoop?

28. Who left the home: husband or wife?

29. Did the children leave too?

30. If you left the home, what did you tell the children?

31. Did the partner who left return to live in the home: once [y/n] or more than once [y/n]?

32. If yes, what affect did this have on the children? Can you give an example?

33. Did you at any time consider staying together for the 'sake of the children' or 'until they are older'? [y/n]

34. Have you kept in contact with your in-laws? [y/n]

35. Do the children see them? [y/n]

36. Has your partner kept in touch with your parents? [y/n]

37. Did either parents try to influence any decisions? [y/n]

38. Have you felt supported by either or both lots of parents? [y/n]

39. Have the children felt supported by either or both lots of grandparents? [y/n]

40. What was the immediate reaction of family and friends about the separation? [y/n]

41. Did you consult your family doctor for you or the children at this time for any reason? [y/n]
    If yes, please state why?

42. Did *you* suffer from any of the following:
    Lack of appetite:
      Immediately [y/n] six months on [y/n] now [y/n]
    Bingeing:
      Immediately [y/n] six months on [y/n] now [y/n]
    Sleep problems:
      Immediately [y/n] six months on [y/n] now [y/n]
    Depression:
      Immediately [y/n] six months on [y/n] now [y/n]
    Lack of self-esteem:
      Immediately [y/n] six months on [y/n] now [y/n]
    Grief:
      Immediately [y/n] six months on [y/n] now [y/n]
    Excessive smoking:
      Immediately [y/n] six months on [y/n] now [y/n]
    Excessive drinking:
      Immediately [y/n] six months on [y/n] now [y/n]
    Murderous rage:
      Immediately [y/n] six months on [y/n] now [y/n]
    Suicidal thoughts:
      Immediately [y/n] six months on [y/n] now [y/n]

43. How do you feel the separation affected the children:
    Poor sleep patterns:
      Immediately [y/n] six months on [y/n] now [y/n]
    Nightmares:
      Immediately [y/n] six months on [y/n] now [y/n]
    Bed-wetting:
      Immediately [y/n] six months on [y/n] now [y/n]
    Food phobias:
      Immediately [y/n] six months on [y/n] now [y/n]

Lack of enthusiasm . . .
. . . in learning:
Immediately [y/n] six months on [y/n] now [y/n]
. . . in play:
Immediately [y/n] six months on [y/n] now [y/n]
Depression:
Immediately [y/n] six months on [y/n] now [y/n]
Regression:
Immediately [y/n] six months on [y/n] now [y/n]
Socially affected in any way:
Immediately [y/n] six months on [y/n] now [y/n]
Anger or aggressive behaviour:
Immediately [y/n] six months on [y/n] now [y/n]

44. Have you been asked any of the following by your children, either directly or indirectly? If yes, how did you answer them – please add your comments:
Where is Daddy? [y/n]
Is he coming home? [y/n]
Why has he gone? [y/n]
Doesn't he love me any more? [y/n]
Doesn't he love you any more? [y/n]
Does he love somebody else? [y/n]
Is it something I did? [y/n]
Is it something I didn't do? [y/n]
Is it something you did? [y/n]
Can I see him [or her]? [y/n]
Car I speak to him [or her]? [y/n]
I don't want to see him [or her], please don't make me . . . [y/n]
Why do I have to go and see him [or her]? [y/n]
Please let Daddy [or Mummy] come home . . . [y/n]
Daddy [or Mummy] says you are horrible . . . [y/n]
Daddy [or Mummy] lets me . . . [y/n]
I want Daddy [or Mummy] *now* . . . I'm sick [y/n]
I want both of you . . . [y/n]
I hate Daddy [or Mummy] . . . [y/n]
I hate you . . . [y/n]

Why doesn't Daddy [or Mummy] want to see me? [y/n]
Is he [or she] coming back? [y/n]
Can I go and live with Daddy [Mummy]? [y/n]
Why are you getting a divorce? [y/n]

45. Did you and/or your partner consider seeing or actually did see a mediator? [y/n]
    If yes, did it help? [y/n]
    If no, why did you not see a mediator?

46. Did you seek any help from a therapist or counsellor? [y/n]
    If so, did it help? [y/n]

47. Did you seek help from a child therapist or psychologist?
    If so, did it help? [y/n]

48. How was access between you and your partner decided?

49. Did it go as planned? [y/n]

50. Were the children old enough to be counsulted over access? [y/n]
    If yes, did you consult them? [y/n]

51. Was there a custody battle? [y/n]

52. Have the arrangements over access improved or deteriorated?

53. If *you* left the home how do you think your partner would have answered the question, 'Where's Daddy [Mummy]?'

54. Is there anything else you would like to add – anything not covered by the above? If so please write below or on a separate sheet of paper.

# Appendix II

# *Resources*

---

## Psychotherapy and counselling

### *For adults*

British Association of Psychotherapists
37 Mapesbury Road, London NW2 4HJ     0181 452 9823
*Trains adult and child psychoanalytic psychotherapists.*
*Contact Clinical Service for consultation and referral to a therapist.*

British Confederation of Psychotherapists
37a Mapesbury Road, London NW2 4HJ     0181 830 5173
*Holds a register of psychotherapists.*

British Association for Counselling
37a Sheep Street, Rugby, Warwickshire CV21 3BX
*Contact for a list of accredited counsellors.*     01788 578328

Guild of Psychotherapists
19b Thornton Hill, London SW19 4HU     0181 947 0730
*Contact for referral for psychoanalytic psychotherapy; also a training*
*organisation.*

Institute of Psychotherapy and Social Studies
18 Laurier Road, London NW5 1SG     0181 446 2434
*Contact for referral to a psychotherapist.*

London Centre for Psychotherapy
19 Fitzjohn's Avenue, London NW3 5JY     0171 435 0873
*Contact for referral to a psychotherapist: also a training organisation.*

NAFSIYAT
278 Seven Sisters Road, London N4 2HY     0171 263 4130
*Inter-cultural therapy and counselling.*

Relate (*Previously* Marriage Guidance)
Herbert Gray College, Little Church Street,
Rugby CV21 3AP     01788 573241
*See telephone book for local numbers.*

Scottish Institute of Human Relations
56 Albany Street, Edinburgh EH1 3QR     0131 556 0924
*Contact for referral to a psychotherapist.*

Westminster Pastoral Foundation
23 Kensington Square, London W8 5HN     0171 937 6956
*Contact for referral to a counsellor: also a training organisation.*

# For children

British Association of Psychotherapists
37 Mapesbury Road, London NW2 4HJ     0181 452 9823
*Consultations and psychoanalytic psychotherapy for children, adults and families.*

Children's Counselling Service
Family & Divorce Centre, 162 Tenison Road,
Cambridge CB1     01223 460136
*Counselling for children under 19 who are experiencing difficulties relating to a present or past parental divorce or separation.*

Anna Freud Centre
21 Maresfield Gardens, London NW3 5SH     0171 794 2313
*Psychotherapy for families and children.*

Child and Family Guidance Clinic
*Ask GP for details*

Institute of Family Therapy
43 New Cavendish Street,
London W1M 7RG     0171 935 1651
*Help for couples to work out their family problems.*

Tavistock Clinic, Adolescent Department/Department
for Children & Families
120 Belsize Lane, London NW3 5BA          0171 435 7111

Child Support Agency
*Enquiry line for maintenance.*          0345 133 133

Coram Meeting Place & Coram Contact Centre
40 Brunswick Square,
London WC1N 1AZ          0171 278 2424

ChildLine
Freepost 1111, London N1 0BL          0800 1111
*For children requiring counselling.*

Children's Legal Centre
20 Compton Terrace, London W1 2UN          0120 687 3820

Invalid Children's Aid Nationwide
1–3 Dufferin Street, London EC1          0171 374 4422

Cerebral Palsy Helpline          0800 626 216

# Feminist psychotherapy and counselling
Birmingham Women's Therapy Centre
The Lodge, 53 Queensbridge Road, Moseley,
Birmingham B13 8QD          0121 442 2241

Psychotherapy Referral Service
(South London)
222 South Norwood Hill, SW25 6AS          0181 711 2311
*(Correspondence only.)*

Women's Therapy Centre
6 Manor Gardens, London N7 6SZ          0171 263 6200

Women's Counselling and Therapy Services
Oxford Chambers, Oxford Place,
Leeds LSI 3AX                                    0113 245 57 25

# Mediation/contact centres

Coram Meeting Place & Coram Contact Centre
Gregory House, 48 Mecklenburgh Square,
London WCIN 1NU                                  0171 278 2424

National Network of Access & Child Contact Centres
St Andrews United Reform Church, Goldsmith Street,
Nottingham NG1 5JT                               01159 484557
*130 centres throughout the country.*

Family Mediators Association                     01273 747750

National Family Mediation,
9 Tavistock Place, London WC1H 9SN               0171 383 5993

Divorce Mediation & Counselling Service
38 Ebury Street, London SW1                       0171 730 2422

# USEFUL ORGANISATIONS

# General

Carlton Cards
Mill Street East, Dewsbury, West Yorkshire       01924 465200

The Cheltenham Group
Cross Winds, Carron Lane, Midhurst, West Sussex GU29 9LB
*A pro-family men's organisation to influence government policy.*

Dr Adriana Marian B LCH
Drakefield Homeopathic Centre,
122A Drakefield Road, SW17 8RR                   0181 672 5253
*Homeopathic Doctor*

Dignity
16 Brixham Close, Horston Grange,
Nuneaton CV11 6YT                            01203 350312
*An organization which supports those confronted with suspected or
confirmed adultery.*

Family Contact Line,
30 Church Street, Altrincham,
Cheshire WA14 4DW                            0161 941 4011

Families Need Fathers
134 Curtain Road, London EC2A 3AR        0171 613 5060
*A national society providing advice on children's issues for separated
and divorced parents, including unmarried parents of either sex.*

Samaritans Help Line
46 Marshall Street, London SW1V 1LR          0345 909090

Salvation Army
Central Office, 101 Queen Victoria Street,
EC4P 4EP                                     0171 236 5222

Families Law Action Group
Cross Winds, Caron Lane, Midhurst,
West Sussex GU29 9LB                         01730 815347
*An organisation dedicated to the reconstruction of legal marriages.*

Family Welfare Association
501–505 Kingsland Road, Dalston,
London E8 4AU                                0171 254 6251

# For single parents and their children
Gingerbread Association for One Parent Families
16–17 Clerkenwell Close, London EC1R OAA  0171 336 8183

Gingerbread Scotland,
Maryhill Community Hall, 304 Maryhill Road,
Glasgow G20 7YE                                    0141 353 0989

Gingerbread Northern Ireland,
169 University Street, Belfast BT7 1HR          01232 234568

National Council for One Parent Families
255 Kentish Town Road, London NW5 2LX    0171 267 1361

Refuge
PO Box 855, London W4 4DH          Crisis Line 0181 995 4430

Reunite, National Council for Abducted Children
PO Box 4, London WC1X 3DX       Advice Line 0171 404 8356

Singlescape
18 Woolverstone Close, Suffolk IP2 9RY
*Postal support/self-help, penfriend group.*

Wel-Care
(See local telephone directory)
*For support of single parents.*

# For prisoners' families

Federation of Prisoners' Families Support Group
Cambridge House, Cambridge Grove,
London W6 OLE                                      0181 741 4578

Prisoners' Advice Service
57 Chalton Street, London NW1 1HY              0171 388 8586

Prisoners' Families & Friends Service
20 Trinity Street, London SE1 1DB              0171 403 4091
*Provides support and advice for prisoners' and their families.*

# For military families
Combat Stress
Broadway House, The Broadway, Wimbledon
London SW19 1RL                           0181 543 6333
*Provides help for military families.*

## USEFUL MAGAZINES AND BOOKS

# Magazines
Divorces
*A magazine for unattached men and women and their children.*

Single Again                              0181 749 3745
*Subscription-only magazine, which offers practical advice to singles.
Also puts people in touch with each other.*

# Books
**For children:**

| | |
|---|---|
| *Dinosaurs Divorce* | L.K. Brown & M. Brown (Collins) |
| *Step by Wicked Step* | Anne Fine (Hamish Hamilton) |
| *Flour Babies* | Anne Fine (Puffin) |
| *Goggle-eyes* | Anne Fine (Puffin) |
| *Madam Doubtfire* | Anne Fine (Puffin) |
| *The Boys & Girls Book About Divorce* | Richard Gardner MD (Bantam) |
| *Buddy* | Nigel Hinton (Puffin) |
| *Ruth has Two Homes* | Ursula Kirchberg |
| *Worlds Apart* | Jill Murphy |
| *Henry's Leg* | Ann Pilling (Puffin) |
| *We Don't all Live with Mum and Dad* | National Council for One Parent Families |

**For adults: fiction and non-fiction**

| | |
|---|---|
| *An Unsentimental Journey* | Vera Cowie (Mandarin) |
| *Touching from a Distance* | Deborah Curtis (Faber and Faber) |
| *To My Ex-Husband* | Susan Dundon |
| *The Blessing* | Nancy Mitford (Penguin) |

*The One That Got Away*          Christ Ryan (Century)

*The Good Divorce*      Constance Ahrons (Bloomsbury)

*Who Can I Talk To?*  Judy Cooper & Jenny Lewis (Hodder and Stoughton)

*Talking to a Stranger*   Lindsay Knight (Hodder and Stoughton)

*The Relate Guide to Starting Again*   Sarah Litvinoff (Vermillion)

# Index

235